D0363670

# Moulinex

# THE FOOD PROCESSOR COOK BOOK

# Moulinex

# THE FOOD PROCESSOR COOK BOOK

## Mary Norwak

Ward Lock Limited · London

First published in Great Britain in 1980
by Ward Lock Limited, 82 Gower Street,
London WC1E 6EQ, a Pentos Company

Reprinted 1981, 1982

Designed by Chris Walker
Photography by Barry Bullough
Food for photography selected and prepared
by Kingsway Public Relations
Line illustrations by
Drawing Attention/Robert Burns

Text filmset in Plantin

Printed by Graficas Reunidas SA, Madrid, Spain

**British Library Cataloguing in Publication Data**

Norwak, Mary
    Moulinex, the food processor cookbook..
    1. Food processor cookery
    I. Title
    641.5'89      TX840.F6

ISBN 0 – 7063 – 5991 – 7

# Contents

# Introduction

Many kitchen machines have been described as revolutionary, but few can have lived up to that reputation as well as the food processor. Ever since primitive man discovered that the application of fire improved the raw foods he had previously eaten, cooks have been working long hours to prepare ingredients. Traditionally mixtures were creamed with a bare hand, eggs were whisked with twigs or forks, and hard ingredients were chopped with knives.

Simple inventions came slowly to the kitchen, and as late as the end of the eighteenth century a servant could spend 3 hours beating a cake mixture. The nineteenth century saw the development of semi-mechanical whisks, mincers and choppers, but it was not until the middle of the twentieth century that the electric mixer began to appear on kitchen worktops. It was now possible for a cook to mix cakes quickly, rub fat in to make pastry, whip cream and whisk egg whites, eliminating cumbersome tasks and saving endless hours in the kitchen. Gradually, the machines sprouted a whole range of attachments, with devices for chopping, grating and slicing. There were juice extractors, coffee grinders, colanders and sieves, cream makers and even an attachment for grinding corn for home breadmakers, and it might have been assumed that no keen cook could wish for further developments.

The major snag with such mixers has however been the size of a really efficient machine and the storage of a wide range of attachments, which has often led to the machine being tucked away in a cupboard and the attachments rarely being used. The revolutionary food processor has eliminated these problems in a masterly fashion. The basic machine is compact – designed to stand on a small area or worktop. With a choice of two blades, foods may be chopped, ground, mixed and blended in a lidded bowl which prevents ingredients being spilled during processing. A series of discs extends the machine's range so that ingredients may be grated, sliced, shredded or chipped.

This book has been specially written to accompany the Moulinex Maxima and the Moulinex Multichef, versatile food processors that are simple to operate and easy to clean. The amateur cook will find them an encouragement to prepare quite complicated recipes; the experienced or professional cook will welcome the speed with which they operate, and both will enjoy the excellent results which are achieved.

Before trying the recipes, spend a little time getting to know the food processor and trying each of its functions, and adapting to the speed and efficiency of the machine. Soon it will take the place of another pair of hands in the kitchen, and you will find yourself using it dozens of times each day.

*Recipes for main meals will serve 4 people.*
*It is important to follow either the metric or the Imperial measures in any one recipe. All spoon measures are level.*

# 1. How the Machine Works

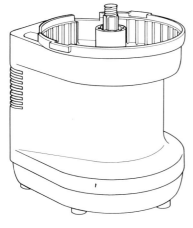

The Maxima food processor has an automatic 2-speed selector which is regulated by the blade or disc selected. The lower speed (1200 revs per minute) is for mixing, kneading, whisking and processing fruit and vegetables. The higher speed (4200 revs per minute) is for chopping.

Safety has been a major concern of the designers. The machine has a double security device which prevents the motor from working unless the cover is in position. The cover cannot be removed unless the system is switched off.

*Parts of the Machine*
*Bowl* fits easily on to the drive shaft of the motor unit without twisting or locking devices.

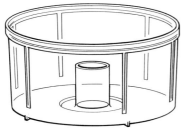

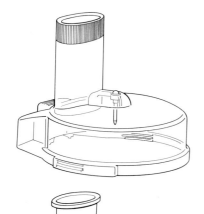

*Cover* fits on to the bowl. It has a release button which should be pressed to free the lock. Plastic guides on the cover have to be lined up with the slots round the top rim of the motor base and then the cover has to be turned so that it is seated firmly. The lock comes into action when the switch button on the cover is pressed.

*Pusher* is used to press foods down the feeder tube when grating, slicing, shredding or chipping. It should be kept in the feeder tube when the tube is not in use.

*Plastic blade* fits on to the drive shaft inside the bowl for mixing and kneading.

*Metal blade* fits on to the drive shaft inside the bowl for chopping.

*Whisk attachment* fits on the drive shaft with the whisks downwards, for whipping cream and whisking egg whites.

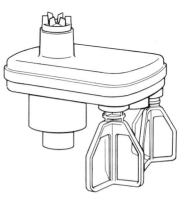

*Cutting disc A/C* is for grating finely or coarsely according to the side used. To fit the disc put the *disc drive* (1) on the shaft in the bowl. Put on the disc, required side up, and secure with *retaining nut* (2). Side A will grate carrots, cheese, etc., finely. Side C with larger holes will grate/slice vegetables more coarsely and produce 'long' potato chips.

*Cutting disc D* is for fine slicing and shredding, and can be used to make potato crisps. Fit it in the same way as disc A/C.

*Cutting disc E* will make large potato chips. Fit it in the same way as disc A/C.

*Cutting disc H* is for thicker slicing and shredding of vegetables, salad ingredients, fruits and sausages such as salami. Fit in the same way as disc A/C.

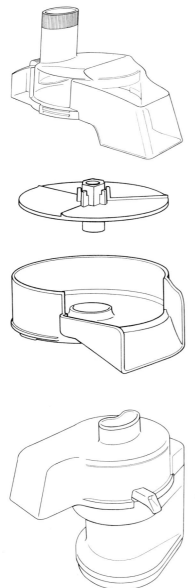

*Ejector cover, disc and bowl* (left) may be used in conjunction with the cutting discs so that processed vegetables can be ejected from the machine. This is a useful attachment if large quantities have to be prepared as it saves emptying the processor bowl a number of times.

*Spatula* (right) is used to scrape down the sides of the bowl between processing, and for taking processed food out of the bowl.

*Blender attachment* (right) fits directly on to the drive shaft and can then be locked into position before use. The blending process is activated by a button on top of the handle.

*Juice extractor attachment* (left) fits on to the bowl in place of the cover, and fruit or vegetables are inserted through the feeder tube.

## Maintenance

Because it is compact, the food processor need not be tucked away in a cupboard. Keep it permanently on a worktop where it will be used many times a day for all kinds of food preparation. Keep the metal blade, cutting discs and any other attachments in a cupboard above the machine, safely out of the reach of children.

The Maxima is easy to clean. Simply wipe the motor base with a damp cloth and then dry well (do not immerse in water). Wash other components in warm water and detergent, rinse and dry thoroughly.

### Assembling and Processing

Full instructions are contained in a special booklet in every Maxima box. Please read this booklet carefully so that you are familiar with the operation of your processor. As with all machines there are some do's and don'ts. Knowing them will not only ensure that you get the most out of food processing, but will also mean that you use the machine safely and wisely.

## The New Moulinex Multichef

The Maxima has now been joined by a new Moulinex food processor – the Multichef. The Multichef is designed with the emphasis on speed, simplicity and compactness. It chops, mixes, kneads, grates, blends and whisks – all the everyday jobs that can take up so much time. And it does all these with the minimum of attachments. So you can race through recipes and have a full meal under way in minutes. In fact, with the Multichef, it's no sooner said than done.

### Adapting recipes

The recipes in this book were designed for the Maxima. However, they all work just as well for the Multichef, because the Multichef carries out *all the functions* of the Maxima. There is only one exception to this, which is that the Multichef does not have the facility for juice extraction.

Where recipes require blending, please note that although the Multichef does not have a blending attachment, blending is extremely well-performed by the metal blade in the bowl provided. (Please bear in mind, though, that its $1\frac{1}{4}$ pint capacity cannot be exceeded).

Where a plastic blade is stipulated, the Multichef's metal blade will perform the same functions just as well – mixing for cakes or kneading bread, for instance.

Please note that where recipes refer to discs by a letter, they concern the Maxima. If you own a Multichef, just use the equivalent disc.

Finally, the recipes which follow cover a wide range of basic dishes. If you want to adapt any of your favourite recipes for either the Maxima or the Multichef, follow the general guidelines given in the appropriate section of the book which indicate how ingredients should be processed. The recipes in each section also indicate the total weight of ingredients which can be processed – it may be necessary to halve your own recipe, or to process the ingredients in two or more batches.

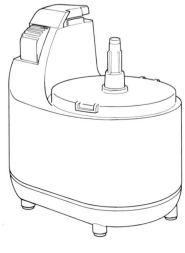

### Parts of the Machine

*Body of machine*   The Multichef has one speed which caters for all its functions. Like the Maxima, great importance has been placed on safety and there is a similar double-security device.

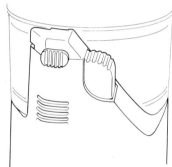

*Pulse and Locking action*   The Multichef has a pulse button which you just press and release for easy action. But there is also a locking button which enables it to work continuously for longer functions such as whisking.

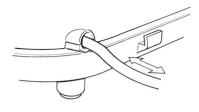

*Retractable cord*   The electric cord is retractable for easier storage and extra safety in the kitchen.

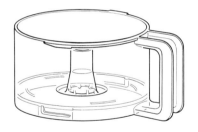

*Bowl*   The bowl fits simply onto the drive shaft on the body of the machine. It has a handle for your convenience, and because it is transparent there is clear visibility when processing.

*Cover*   Also transparent, it fits neatly onto the bowl.

*Pusher*   A removable pusher is used to press food down the grater. It should remain in the hopper when not in use.

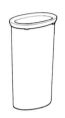

*Metal Blade*   The Multichef has one metal blade, which fits onto the drive shaft in bowl. It is designed for chopping, mixing, kneading and blending.

*Whisk attachment* (optional)   Fits onto the drive shaft – for whipping cream or whisking egg whites.

*Slicing disc*   The stalk of the disc simply drops onto the drive shaft for slicing vegetables.

*Grating disc*   Again, the stalk of the disc fits onto the drive shaft for tasks such as grating cheese.

*Chipping disc*   A chipping disc is available as an optional extra.

*Spatula*   The Multichef has a plastic spatula for handling processed food hygienically.

# 2. A-Z of Ingredients and Processes

*Batter*

Smooth, light, creamy batter is easily produced for pancakes, Yorkshire pudding, drop scones, etc. Fit the plastic blade and put the flour and eggs into the bowl. With the machine running, add milk slowly through the feeder tube. Large quantities of batter should be processed in the blender attachment.

*Blending*

A food processor will produce smooth soups, sauces, etc. very quickly. Use the metal blade to purée vegetable soups, and the plastic blade to blend sauces. To prevent splashing when puréeing soups, strain off some of the stock before processing the vegetables, then return the stock to the purée. If a very smooth texture is required or there is a lot of liquid in the mixture use the blender attachment.

*Breadmaking*

A small quantity of excellent bread dough may be made in the food processor, using the plastic blade. The yeast is mixed evenly through the dough and the machine saves tiring kneading. The dough may also be returned to the machine for the knocking back stage (or second kneading) that takes place after the dough has risen the first time and before it is proved (or left to rise a second time). The food processor prepares enough dough for a 450 g (1 lb) loaf or 8–10 rolls – ideal for the small family. As the processing is so quick and effortless, however, little extra time is involved in making up subsequent quantities of dough for a larger bake-in.

*Butters*

The fast action of the food processor whips up butter lightly using the plastic blade. As well as preparing butter for cakes and icings, the machine may be used for making flavoured butters (with the addition of herbs, essences, etc.) for garnishing or spreading.

### Cakes
Cake mixtures are light and fluffy when made in a food processor, using the plastic blade. Cakes made by the 'creaming' method are best made as one-step cakes, using soft margarine and putting all the ingredients into the processor at the beginning of processing. Cakes made by the 'rubbed-in' method may be made with the processor if the dry ingredients and fat are first processed and liquids introduced through the feeder tube while the machine is running. Whisked sponges cannot be made in the processor.

### Cheese
Cheese may be quickly grated with disc A, or it may be chopped in small pieces with the metal blade. Chopped cheese will melt quickly into sauces.

### Chips
Potato chips are little trouble as disc E prepares the potatoes in seconds.

### Chocolate
Chocolate will melt quickly if grated with disc A, or chopped with the metal blade. Grated chocolate is also useful for garnishing, and chopped chocolate may be incorporated into cake and biscuit mixtures instead of commercially prepared chocolate pieces.

### Chopping
The metal blade can be used for chopping a wide range of ingredients, including cheese, chocolate, meat, fruit and vegetables. Ingredients should first be cut into small pieces. The machine chops coarsely, then very finely and finally processes into purée. Because the chopping process is extremely fast it must be carefully controlled by operating the machine for only a few seconds at a time otherwise foods will be over-processed.

### Choux Pastry
The food processor makes superbly light choux pastry for éclairs, etc. When the basic mixture has been prepared and

cooled it should be placed in the processor bowl with the plastic blade. The eggs can then be added one at a time through the feeder tube while the machine is running. Choux pastry made by this method is featherlight and crisp.

### Cooked Meat
The metal blade on the food processor will chop cooked meat coarsely or finely, or will reduce it to a purée suitable for spreading, and this makes economical use of small quantities of leftover meat. Fat, gristle and skin should be trimmed before processing, and the meat should be cut into small pieces.

### Cream
Whipping or double cream may be whipped to soft or stiff peaks with the whisk attachment.

### Crumbs
Bread, cakes and biscuits can be quickly turned into crumbs in the food processor with the metal blade. Cut or break bread, cake or biscuits into small pieces and control processing carefully to the exact coarseness of crumb required. Over-processing will result in a fine powder which is unsuitable for use in recipes.

### Fruit
Raw or cooked fruit may be chopped or made into a purée with the metal blade or the blender attachment. Fruit juice may be extracted with the juice extractor attachment.

### Grating
A single disc may be used for grating cheese, chocolate and vegetables. The disc is reversible to produce fine or coarse results.

### Herbs
Fresh herbs such as mint or parsley may be quickly and finely chopped, using the metal blade. It is a good idea to chop a large quantity of herbs for storage in the refrigerator or freezer.

### Ice
Crushed ice for drinks may be prepared in the processor, using the metal blade.

### Juice

Fresh fruit and vegetable juices can be prepared with the juice extractor attachment. These can be used for drinks or recipes.

### Leftovers

There is no need to waste leftovers when a food processor is available. Cooked meat can be turned into second-day dishes or spreads; cooked vegetables with stock or gravy can be made the basis of soup as can vegetable oddments from the storage bin. Cooked fruit may be made into a purée or fool, perhaps with leftover custard or cream. Hard ends of cheese may be chopped or grated for recipes or for storage in the freezer; bread, cake and biscuits become useful crumbs for immediate use or freezer storage.

### Meringue

The whisk attachment can be used to make meringue. Whisk the egg whites to stiff peaks. With the motor running add half the sugar through the feeder tube and process for 20 seconds. Fold in the remaining sugar with a spoon.

### Mincing

The metal blade of the food processor will finely chop raw or cooked meats. Fruit and vegetables, too, can be processed for use in chutney or mincemeat.

### Mousses

The various processes involved in making a mousse can be effortlessly achieved with a food processor. Sauce or custard may be smoothed, cream whipped, egg whites whisked and garnishes chopped so that even a complicated recipe may be easily prepared.

### Mushrooms

Mushrooms may be chopped coarsely or finely with the metal blade or they may be sliced with disc H. It is best to use firm button mushrooms as these will process neatly without squashing.

### Nuts

All kinds of nuts may be chopped coarsely or finely with the metal blade. They can also be processed almost as finely as flour, when necessary, for cakes and biscuits.

## Onions

For processing, onions should be peeled and cut in quarters or eighths according to size before being chopped coarsely or finely with the metal blade. They may also be grated with disc C, or sliced with discs D or H. Even a large quantity of onions may be quickly processed without causing tears.

## Pastry

Dough made in a food processor is excellent as it receives little handling. Combine flour and fat(s) in the bowl and process with the plastic blade until the mixture is like coarse breadcrumbs. Use the metal blade if fat is particularly hard and cold. Add liquid through the feeder tube with the machine switched on until the dough forms a firm smooth ball round the blade. The fat should be cool and firm and block margarine is excellent for the purpose. Water should be ice cold and added slowly as flours vary slightly (some absorb more liquid than others), so always keep back 1–2 tablespoons in case the dough forms more quickly than expected. Pastry made in the processor will not be warm, so should not need chilling, but it is advisable to chill sweet shortcrust pastry and flaky pastry which are a little more difficult to handle. Hot water crust pastry can also be quickly made.

## Purées

Purées can be quickly made by using the metal blade, but the texture will remain a little coarse. For a finer texture, use the blender attachment.

## Raw Meat

Raw meat of all kinds, including offal, can be coarsely or finely chopped with the metal blade. It takes about 15 seconds to chop 450 g (1 lb) meat evenly and finely. This processing is ideal for making burgers or steak tartare, and is invaluable when preparing pâtés.

## Salads

A food processor is a particular advantage to those wishing to vary the type and texture of salads. Raw vegetables may be chopped with the metal blade, or grated, shredded or sliced with the various discs. Cooked vegetables may be chopped coarsely for adding to mayonnaise or salad cream. All types of salad dressings may be made in the processor.

## Sauces

In addition to salad dressings, a wide variety of sauces may be prepared in the food processor. A sauce may be made by a conventional method and then smoothed in the processor bowl, using the plastic blade (large quantities should be processed in the blender attachment). Flour-based sauces may be mixed in the processor *before* heating which speeds up the cooking and keeps the sauce smooth. Emulsified sauces, which require the slow addition of oil or melted butter, can be safely made in the processor as the liquid can be poured very slowly through the feeder tube.

## Slicing

Even slices can be produced with discs D or H. Vegetables, fruit and sausages are just a few of the foods that can be quickly sliced.

## Soufflés

Very light soufflés are easily made as all the ingredients except the egg whites can be combined and processed with the plastic blade. The egg whites can be stiffly whisked with the whisk attachment.

## Suet

Use the metal blade to chop suet cut from a freezer carcase or other meat.

## Vegetables

Vegetables can be quickly chopped, grated, sliced or shredded in a food processor. Vegetable purées may also be prepared by creaming cooked vegetables with butter or cream.

## Whisking

The whisk attachment may be used for whipping cream or whisking egg whites. When processing egg whites, the bowl and whisk must be scrupulously clean, dry and free from grease; and it is best to process without the pusher fitted into the feeder tube, as this will increase the supply of air to the egg whites.

# 3. Soups

A bowl of home-made soup is delicious and can make a meal on its own, or supplement a light salad meal. In hot weather, iced soup is refreshing and stimulates the appetite. At any time, the combination of vegetables and stock with protein in the form of cheese, meat or fish is both nourishing and inexpensive.

The food processor can speed up soup-making in a number of ways. Previously, a soup might be made from a number of ingredients which had to be laboriously cut or grated by hand. Now the food processor chops, shreds, slices and grates in a matter of seconds, and a saucepan of soup can be very quickly assembled. If a smooth, creamy soup is required, sieving can be eliminated by using the metal blade or blender attachment, after the ingredients have been cooked and the flavours blended. For the economical cook, the food processor transforms leftover vegetables, ends of cheese, and oddments of bread into soup which can be prepared in just a few minutes.

To prepare soup ingredients, chop vegetables with the metal blade or slice or grate with the appropriate discs. Chop garnishing herbs with the metal blade and grate cheese with a disc. Prepare quick croûtons by tearing up pieces of bread roughly and processing with the metal blade just long enough to produce large 'crumbs' which can be fried in hot fat.

# Cod Chowder

675 g (1½ lb) cod (or haddock)
600 ml (1 pint) water
1 large onion
50 g (2 oz) butter
2 large potatoes
3 celery sticks
25 g (1 oz) plain flour
1·5 litres (2½ pints) milk
1 tablespoon Worcestershire
  sauce
salt and pepper
1 sprig of parsley

Cover the fish with the water and simmer for 20 minutes. Drain fish, retaining the cooking liquid. Remove skin and bones from the fish, and flake the fish with a fork. Peel the onion and chop it finely (metal blade). Melt the butter in a pan and cook the onion over low heat for 5 minutes until soft and golden. Peel the potatoes and wash and trim the celery. Chop the potatoes and celery coarsely (metal blade). Add to the onions and stir over low heat for 5 minutes. Stir in the flour and cook for 1 minute. Gradually work in the milk and then add the flaked fish and half the reserved cooking liquid. Bring to the boil and then simmer for 15 minutes. Season with Worcestershire sauce, salt and pepper, and simmer for 5 minutes. Chop the parsley (metal blade) and sprinkle over the chowder before serving.

# Queen Victoria Soup

1 small onion
25 g (1 oz) butter
2 celery sticks
100 g (4 oz) button mushrooms
900 ml (1½ pints) chicken stock
100 g (4 oz) cooked chicken
100 g (4 oz) cooked ham
1 tablespoon quick-cooking
  tapioca
salt and pepper
pinch of ground nutmeg
pinch of dried sage
2 hard-boiled eggs, shelled
1 sprig of parsley
150 ml (¼ pint) single cream

Peel the onion and chop finely (metal blade). Melt the butter in a pan and stir the onion over low heat for 5 minutes until soft and golden. Wash, trim and chop the celery (metal blade). Wipe the mushrooms and slice thickly (disc H). Add to the onion and cook over low heat for 10 minutes. Add the chicken stock and simmer for 5 minutes. Chop the chicken and ham finely (metal blade). Add to the stock with the tapioca, salt, pepper, nutmeg and sage. Cover and simmer for 20 minutes. Chop the eggs and parsley finely (metal blade). Just before serving, stir the eggs, parsley and cream into the soup and reheat without boiling.

# Garbure

Soak the beans in water to cover for 3 hours. Skin the tomatoes by dipping them in boiling water. Cut them in quarters and discard the pips. Chop the flesh coarsely (metal blade). Peel the carrots, turnips, potatoes and garlic clove and chop coarsely (metal blade). Shred the cabbage (disc H). Drain the beans and put in a pan with the stock. Simmer for 1 hour. Melt the butter and stir in the vegetables. Cook over low heat for 5 minutes. Add the stock and beans and season with salt and pepper. Bring to the boil, cover and simmer for 30 minutes. Cool slightly and then blend until smooth (blender attachment). Return to the pan and reheat, adjusting seasoning to taste. Just before serving, toast the French bread slices on one side. Beat the egg lightly in a bowl. Grate the cheese (disc A) and mix with the egg. Spread on the untoasted sides of the bread and toast until golden and bubbling. Put one piece in each serving bowl and pour in the soup.

50 g (2 oz) haricot beans
2 tomatoes
2 carrots
2 turnips
450 g (1 lb) potatoes
1 garlic clove
350 g (12 oz) white cabbage
1 litre (1¾ pints) beef stock
50 g (2 oz) butter
salt and pepper
4 thick slices French bread
1 egg
50 g (2 oz) Cheddar cheese

# Country Carrot Soup

Peel the carrots, potatoes and onions. Slice the carrots (disc H). Quarter the potatoes and the onions and chop them (metal blade). Melt the butter in a heavy-based pan and cook the onions gently for 5 minutes, stirring well. Add the carrots and potatoes, and continue cooking for 10 minutes, stirring often. Add the stock, salt, pepper, bay leaf, thyme and 1 sprig of parsley. Bring to the boil, and then cover and simmer for 25 minutes until the vegetables are soft. Remove the bay leaf, thyme and parsley. Strain off the liquid into a clean pan. Blend the vegetables until smooth and creamy (blender attachment). Add to the liquid in the pan and reheat gently. Chop the remaining parsley (metal blade) and sprinkle on the soup just before serving. If liked, serve with small cubes of toasted or fried bread.

675 g (1½ lb) carrots
450 g (1 lb) potatoes
225 g (8 oz) onions
75 g (3 oz) butter
1·2 litres (2 pints) chicken stock
salt and pepper
1 bay leaf
1 sprig of thyme
3 sprigs of parsley

# Florentine Soup

1 kg (2 lb) fresh spinach
100 g (4 oz) onions
50 g (2 oz) butter
900 ml (1½ pints) chicken stock
salt and pepper
pinch of ground nutmeg
4 tablespoons single cream
50 g (2 oz) Cheddar cheese

Remove the stems from the spinach and wash the leaves thoroughly. Put into a large saucepan and just cover with boiling water. Bring to the boil quickly and drain thoroughly. Cool the spinach completely under running water. This treatment removes the very strong taste from the spinach which many people dislike. Peel the onions and chop finely (metal blade). Melt the butter and stir the onions over low heat for 5 minutes until soft and golden. Drain the spinach thoroughly and add to the pan. Stir well to coat with butter, cover and simmer for 10 minutes. Cool slightly and blend until smooth (blender attachment). Return to the pan with the stock, salt, pepper and nutmeg. Bring to the boil, cover and simmer for 15 minutes. Just before serving, stir in the cream. Grate the cheese (disc A) and sprinkle generously on each portion of soup.

# Cream of Cucumber Soup

2 cucumbers
1 small onion
25 g (1 oz) butter
25 g (1 oz) plain flour
300 ml (½ pint) chicken stock
1 bay leaf
salt and pepper
pinch of ground nutmeg
450 ml (¾ pint) milk
1 sprig of parsley
150 ml (¼ pint) single cream

Peel the cucumbers and slice (disc H). Peel the onion and chop finely (metal blade). Melt the butter in a pan and cook the onion over low heat for 5 minutes, stirring well, until soft and golden. Work in the flour and cook for 2 minutes, stirring well, add the stock and stir well. Add the cucumber slices, bay leaf, salt, pepper and nutmeg. Bring to the boil, then cover and simmer for 10 minutes. Add the milk and simmer for 5 minutes. Cool slightly and then blend until smooth (blender attachment). Cover and chill for 2 hours. Just before serving, chop the parsley (metal blade) and stir into the soup with the cream.

# Lentil Soup with Frankfurters

350 g (12 oz) lentils (or split peas)
6 ripe tomatoes
1 carrot
1 onion
1·7 litres (3 pints) bacon stock
salt and pepper
2 frankfurter sausages

Soak the lentils or split peas for 12 hours in cold water. Skin the tomatoes by dipping them in boiling water. Cut them in quarters and discard the pips. Chop the flesh coarsely (metal blade). Peel the carrot and onion and chop them coarsely (metal blade). Drain the lentils or split peas and put them in a saucepan. Add the tomatoes, carrot and onion. Pour in the bacon stock, add pepper and salt if required. (If the stock is very salty, do not add extra salt.) Bring to the boil, cover and simmer for 1 hour until the lentils are soft. Cool slightly and blend until smooth (blender attachment). Slice the frankfurters in thick pieces and add to the soup. Reheat, adjust seasoning to taste.

# Golden Soup

Peel the onion and chop it finely (metal blade). Heat the butter in a pan and cook the onion over low heat for 5 minutes, stirring well. Skin the tomatoes by dipping them in boiling water. Cut them in quarters and discard the pips. Chop the flesh coarsely (metal blade) and add to the onion mixture. Cook gently for 5 minutes. Slice the carrots (disc D) and add to the tomatoes. Cook for 2 minutes, then add water, salt, sugar, celery salt and pepper. Bring to the boil, cover and simmer for 15 minutes. Cool slightly and blend until smooth (blender attachment). Stir in the orange juice. Reheat if the soup is to be served hot, or chill for cold service. Chop the parsley finely (metal blade) and serve each portion garnished with a sprinkling of parsley.

1 small onion
25 g (1 oz) butter
450 g (1 lb) ripe tomatoes
225 g (8 oz) carrots
450 ml ($\frac{3}{4}$ pint) water
1 teaspoon salt
1 teaspoon sugar
pinch of celery salt
pinch of pepper
150 ml ($\frac{1}{4}$ pint) orange juice
1 sprig of parsley

# Leek and Potato Soup

Wash the leeks thoroughly, remove green tops and slice the white parts (disc H). Keep on one side. Peel the potatoes and slice them (disc H). Melt the butter in a pan and stir the leeks over low heat for 5 minutes. Add the potatoes and continue cooking for 3 minutes, stirring well. Add the stock and bring to the boil. Cover and simmer for 20 minutes. Chop the chives (metal blade). The soup may be served in two ways. *Either* stir in the milk, season to taste, reheat and serve with a garnish of chopped chives *or* blend until smooth (blender attachment) and then reheat with milk and seasoning before serving with chopped chives.

450 g (1 lb) young leeks
450 g (1 lb) potatoes
50 g (2 oz) butter
750 ml (1$\frac{1}{4}$ pints) chicken stock
6 stems of chives
300 ml ($\frac{1}{2}$ pint) milk
salt and pepper

*Vichyssoise*
Follow the instructions as above until the soup has simmered 20 minutes, then blend until smooth (blender attachment). Add milk and seasoning and reheat. Pour into a bowl, cover and chill until serving time. Stir in 150 ml ($\frac{1}{4}$ pint) single cream and serve garnished with chopped chives.

1. Slicing carrot

2. Potatoes ready for chopping

3. Parsley ready for chopping

# Minestrone

75 g (3 oz) dried haricot beans
1·7 litres (3 pints) beef or
  bacon stock
100 g (4 oz) smoked bacon
1 large carrot
1 onion
¼ small cabbage
225 g (8 oz) potatoes
1 garlic clove
225 g (8 oz) canned tomatoes
100 g (4 oz) frozen peas
pinch of dried rosemary
salt and pepper
75 g (3 oz) pasta
3 sprigs of parsley
25 g (1 oz) Parmesan or
  Cheddar cheese

Put the beans into a bowl, cover with cold water and leave to soak overnight. Drain the beans and put them into a pan with the stock. Bring to the boil, cover and simmer for 1 hour. Chop the bacon (metal blade) and heat the pieces in a small pan until the fat runs and the bacon is golden brown. Drain off the excess fat, and put the bacon into the stock. Slice the carrot, onion and cabbage (disc D). Chop the potatoes coarsely (metal blade). Crush the garlic. Add all these vegetables and the garlic to the stock. Add the tomatoes and their juice. Cover and simmer for 35 minutes. Stir in the peas, rosemary, salt and pepper and simmer for 5 minutes. Add pasta shapes or small pieces of macaroni, spaghetti or vermicelli. Cook for 10–12 minutes until pasta is tender. Chop the parsley (metal blade) and grate the cheese (disc A). Serve the soup in a tureen or individual bowls and sprinkle with parsley and cheese.

# Beetroot Soup

350 g (12 oz) cooked beetroot
1 onion
1 celery stick
600 ml (1 pint) beef stock
salt and pepper
1 teaspoon sugar
2 tablespoons lemon juice
1 pickled cucumber
150 ml ($\frac{1}{4}$ pint) soured cream

Peel the beetroot and cut into pieces. Chop coarsely (metal blade) and put into a saucepan. Peel the onion and wash and trim the celery. Chop the onion and celery coarsely (metal blade). Add to the beetroot with the stock, salt, pepper and sugar. Bring to the boil, then cover and simmer for 15 minutes. Cool the soup slightly and then blend until smooth (blender attachment). Add the lemon juice. Reheat if the soup is to be served hot, or chill for cold service. Chop the pickled cucumber finely (metal blade). Serve each portion with a large spoonful of soured cream and a sprinkling of chopped cucumber.

# Fresh Tomato Soup

1 small onion
1 bacon rasher
25 g (1 oz) butter
450 g (1 lb) ripe tomatoes
1 potato
600 ml (1 pint) beef stock
salt and pepper
$\frac{1}{2}$ teaspoon sugar
1 sprig of basil or marjoram
150 ml ($\frac{1}{4}$ pint) double cream
1 teaspoon grated orange rind

Peel the onion and chop finely (metal blade). Derind the bacon and chop coarsely (metal blade). Melt the butter in a pan and stir the onion and bacon over a low heat for 5 minutes. Skin the tomatoes by dipping them in boiling water. Cut them in quarters and discard the pips. Chop the flesh coarsely (metal blade) and add to the onion mixture. Cook gently for 5 minutes. Peel the potato and cut in pieces. Chop coarsely (metal blade) and add to the tomatoes. Add the stock, salt, pepper, sugar and sprig of basil or marjoram. Bring to the boil, then cover and simmer for 30 minutes. Cool slightly and blend until smooth (blender attachment). Reheat gently. Just before serving, whip the cream to soft peaks (whisk attachment). Pour the soup into individual bowls and garnish each with a spoonful of cream sprinkled with a little grated orange rind.

# Cream of Green Pea Soup

If using frozen peas, allow them to thaw until just softened before using. Peel the onion and chop it finely (metal blade). Melt the butter in a pan and cook the onion over low heat, stirring well, for 5 minutes. Add the peas, parsley, salt, sugar, pepper, nutmeg and water. Cover and simmer for 20 minutes. Cool slightly and blend until smooth (blender attachment). Add the milk and blend until mixed. Return to saucepan and reheat gently. Stir in cream and reheat gently without boiling. Chop the mint (metal blade) and garnish the soup.

450 g (1 lb) shelled green peas
 (or frozen peas)
1 small onion
50 g (2 oz) butter
1 sprig of parsley
1 teaspoon salt
1 teaspoon sugar
pinch of pepper
pinch of ground nutmeg
300 ml (½ pint) water
300 ml (½ pint) milk
150 ml (¼ pint) single cream
1 sprig of mint

# Cream of Mushroom Soup

Peel the onion and chop it finely (metal blade). Derind the bacon and chop it coarsely (metal blade). Wipe the mushrooms and slice thickly (disc H). Melt the butter in a pan and cook the onion and bacon over low heat, stirring well, for 5 minutes. Add the mushrooms and stir over low heat for 5 minutes. Stir in the flour and cook for 2 minutes. Add the stock and milk, stir well and bring to the boil. Season with salt and pepper, cover and simmer for 20 minutes. Cool slightly and blend until smooth (blender attachment). Stir in the cream and heat very gently but do not boil. Chop the chives (metal blade) and sprinkle over soup.

1 small onion
1 streaky bacon rasher
225 g (8 oz) mushrooms
25 g (1 oz) butter
25 g (1 oz) plain flour
600 ml (1 pint) chicken stock
300 ml (½ pint) milk
salt and pepper
150 ml (¼ pint) single cream
6 stems of chives

# Cream of Chicken Soup

Peel the onion and carrot. Wash and trim the celery. Slice the onion, carrot and celery (disc D). Melt the butter in a pan and cook the vegetables over low heat, stirring well, for 5 minutes. Work in the flour and continue cooking for 2 minutes. Add the stock, stir well and bring to the boil slowly. Season with salt and pepper, cover and simmer for 20 minutes. Chop the chicken finely (metal blade) and keep on one side. Chop the parsely finely (metal blade). Cool the soup slightly and then blend until smooth (blender attachment). Return to the pan and stir in the chopped chicken. Bring to the boil. Remove from heat, stir in the cream and parsley and serve at once.

1 onion
1 carrot
1 celery stick
25 g (1 oz) butter
25 g (1 oz) plain flour
750 ml (1¼ pints) chicken stock
salt and pepper
100 g (4 oz) cooked chicken
1 sprig of parsley
4 tablespoons single cream

# French Onion Soup

450 g (1 lb) onions
50 g (2 oz) butter
1 tablespoon cooking oil
900 ml (1½ pints) stock
salt and pepper
1 large sprig of parsley
50 g (2 oz) Cheddar cheese
4 thick slices French bread

Peel and quarter the onions and slice them (disc D). Melt butter and oil together in a pan and stir in sliced onions. Cook over low heat until soft and golden but not browned. Add stock, salt and pepper and simmer for 20 minutes. Chop the parsley (metal blade). Grate the cheese (disc A). Toast the bread slices on one side. Sprinkle cheese on the other side and toast until bubbling. Pour the soup into serving bowls and float a toast slice in each.

# Spring Vegetable Soup

2 young carrots
2 young white turnips
1 cabbage lettuce heart
12 baby silver onions
1 sprig of tarragon
900 ml (1½ pints) chicken stock
1 teaspoon sugar
salt and pepper

Scrape the carrots and turnips and chop finely (metal blade). Put into a saucepan. Shred the lettuce heart (disc H) and add to the pan. Peel the onions but leave them whole. Add to the pan with the tarragon, stock, sugar, salt and pepper. Bring to the boil, then cover and simmer for 20 minutes. Remove the tarragon before serving.

# Chilled Avocado Soup

1 large or 2 small avocados
1 teaspoon lemon juice
25 g (1 oz) dill leaves
1 slice onion
900 ml (1½ pints) chicken stock
300 ml (½ pint) single cream
salt and white pepper
paprika pepper

Peel the avocado(s) and remove the stone(s). Cut each into 8 pieces. Put into the bowl with the lemon juice, dill leaves, onion and 300 ml (½ pint) stock. Chop finely (metal blade). Transfer the mixture to the blender attachment. With the motor running, slowly pour in the remaining stock and blend until smooth. Pour into a serving bowl and stir in the cream, salt and pepper. Cover and chill for an hour before serving. Garnish each portion with a small pinch of paprika. Be sure to use white pepper for this soup as a dark pepper will spoil the delicate colour.

# Gazpacho

There are dozens of recipes for this Spanish soup, coming from different regions and families. The most important ingredients are high-quality olive oil and very good bread, preferably home-made. Cut the tomatoes in half and put into a large pan. Peel the onions and slice them (disc H). Peel and crush the garlic. Add onions and garlic to the tomatoes. Cover with water, add the oil, salt and pepper, celery salt, sherry and vinegar and bring to the boil. Cover and simmer for 1 hour. Cool and blend (blender attachment). Put through a sieve to remove pips and skin, and pour into a serving bowl. Chill for at least 2 hours before serving.

To make the garnishes, peel the cucumber and chop coarsely (metal blade). Remove stems, seeds and membranes from peppers and chop the flesh coarsely, mixing the different colours (metal blade). Skin the tomatoes by dipping them in boiling water; cut them in quarters and discard the pips; chop the flesh coarsely (metal blade). Remove crusts from the bread; cut the bread into 1 cm ($\frac{1}{2}$ in) dice and put on a baking sheet; bake at 150 °C/300 °F/Gas Mark 2 for 5 minutes. Put cucumber, peppers, tomatoes and bread into individual serving dishes. Serve the chilled soup with the side dishes for garnishing.

1 kg (2 lb) ripe tomatoes
2 large Spanish onions
2 garlic cloves
4 tablespoons olive oil
salt and pepper
pinch of celery salt
150 ml ($\frac{1}{4}$ pint) dry sherry
1 tablespoon tarragon vinegar

*Garnishes*
1 cucumber
450 g (1 lb) green, red and
　yellow peppers
4 large ripe tomatoes
1 small loaf white bread

# 4. Starters, Spreads and Dips

First courses that are both light and colourful will be sure to whet the appetite for the meal ahead. The work of whipping ingredients and chopping garnishes – to make tempting starters, spreads and dips – is all made so easy with the help of a food processor.

Try making some of the recipes in this section before experimenting with your own favourite ingredients and recipes. Put the solid ingredients in the bowl and chop finely (metal blade). Add the thick soft ingredients such as cream, salad cream or cottage cheese and process until the ingredients are well blended (plastic blade). (For larger quantities use the blender.) Add lemon juice or other liquids last. Always chill dips for at least one hour before serving so that the mixtures will have time to firm up a little.

## Chicken Cannelloni

8 pieces cannelloni pasta
1 onion
1 garlic clove
100 g (4 oz) button mushrooms
2 tablespoons oil
225 g (8 oz) cooked chicken
15 g (½ oz) day-old white bread
25 g (1 oz) Parmesan cheese
1 teaspoon chopped fresh
   marjoram
1 egg
salt and pepper

Bring a large pan of salted water to the boil and put in the pieces of pasta. Stir for a minute so that they do not stick together. Cook for about 10 minutes until just tender. Drain well and leave to cool while preparing the filling.

Peel the onion and garlic and chop finely (metal blade). Wipe the mushrooms and chop coarsely (metal blade). Heat the oil in a pan and cook the onion, garlic and mushrooms for 5 minutes over a low heat stirring well. Cut the chicken into pieces and chop very finely (metal blade). Discard crusts from bread, cut bread into pieces and make into crumbs (metal blade), grate the cheese (disc A). Stir the chicken into the onion mixture with breadcrumbs, cheese and marjoram. Take off the heat and work in the egg, salt and pepper. Cool and then divide the filling between the pieces of pasta. Roll up lengthways. Butter an ovenware dish and arrange the pasta in it.

To make the sauce, mix 40 g (1½ oz) butter, the flour and the milk until smooth (plastic blade). Pour into a pan, bring to the boil and simmer for 3 minutes, stirring all the time. Stir in the cream and heat gently, stirring well. Season with salt, pepper and nutmeg. Spoon over the pasta and dot with flakes of the remaining butter. Grate the cheese (disc A) and sprinkle over the pasta. Bake at 190 °C/375 °F/Gas Mark 5 for 30 minutes. Serve as a first course, or as a main course with green salad and crusty bread.

*Sauce*
50 g (2 oz) butter
40 g (1½ oz) plain flour
300 ml (½ pint) milk
150 ml (¼ pint) single cream
salt and white pepper
pinch of grated nutmeg
25 g (1 oz) Parmesan cheese

# Stuffed Peppers in Tomato Sauce

Bring to the boil a pan of salted water. Remove lids from peppers and set aside. Discard seeds and put peppers into the boiling water. Boil for 5 minutes, drain thoroughly. Grease an ovenware dish and put the peppers in it. Peel the onion and garlic and chop coarsely (metal blade). Derind the bacon and cut the beef into cubes. Add the bacon, beef and chicken livers to the onion and continue processing until the beef is finely chopped. Heat the oil in a pan and cook the meat mixture until lightly browned, stirring well. Season to taste and spoon the mixture into the peppers. Replace the lids lightly on the peppers.

To make the sauce, peel the onion and chop it finely (metal blade). Melt the butter in a pan and fry the onion until soft and golden. Return to the bowl with the remaining ingredients and mix until smooth (plastic blade). Put through a sieve to remove the pips. Put into a pan, bring to the boil and simmer for 5 minutes, stirring all the time. Adjust seasoning if necessary. Pour the sauce over the peppers, cover with a lid or foil and bake at 180 °C/350 °F/Gas Mark 4 for 40 minutes. These peppers are delicious served cold as a first course, but they are also good hot with an accompaniment of savoury rice.

4 green peppers
1 small onion
1 garlic clove
2 rashers streaky bacon
225 g (8 oz) chuck steak
100 g (4 oz) chicken livers
1 tablespoon oil
salt and pepper

*Tomato Sauce*
1 onion
25 g (1 oz) butter
25 g (1 oz) plain flour
400 g (14 oz) canned tomatoes
1 tablespoon tomato purée
1 teaspoon sugar
pinch of dried mixed herbs
salt and pepper

1. Adding egg to milk to make batter

2. Chopping chicken

3. Chopping cheese

# Savoury Stuffed Pancakes

*Pancakes*
300 ml (½ pint) milk
1 egg
pinch of salt
100 g (4 oz) plain flour
fat for frying

*Filling*
175 g (6 oz) cooked chicken
1 small onion
100 g (4 oz) button mushrooms
25 g (1 oz) butter
450 ml (¾ pint) white sauce
  (page 141)
salt and pepper
50 g (2 oz) Cheddar cheese

Mix the milk, egg and salt (blender attachment) for 5 seconds or put ingredients into the bowl and mix for 5 seconds (plastic blade). Tip in the flour and mix until smooth and creamy. Grease an 18 cm (7 in) frying pan lightly and fry 8 thin pancakes. Keep them warm.

To make the filling, chop the chicken finely (metal blade). Keep on one side. Peel the onion and wipe the mushrooms and chop finely (metal blade). Cook the onion and mushroom mixture in the butter until just soft and golden. Stir in the chicken and mix well. Add 150 ml (¼ pint) white sauce, mix well and adjust seasoning to taste. Divide this mixture between the pancakes and roll them up. Arrange in a fireproof dish. Chop the cheese (metal blade) and add to the remaining white sauce, stirring until just melted. Spoon over the pancakes. Put under a hot grill until the sauce is bubbling and golden.

# Stuffed Eggs

8 hard-boiled eggs, shelled
75 g (3 oz) butter
2 tablespoons mayonnaise
100 g (4 oz) peeled prawns
salt and pepper
½ teaspoon curry powder

Cut the eggs in half lengthways and remove the yolks. Soften the butter slightly but do not melt. Put the butter and mayonnaise into the processor bowl with the egg yolks. Reserve 8 prawns and put the rest into the bowl with the salt, pepper and curry powder. Process until smooth (metal blade). Spoon into the egg halves and garnish each with half a prawn.

# Individual Seafood Flans

350 g (12 oz) made shortcrust
    pastry (page 86)
6 spring onions
15 g (½ oz) butter
100 g (4 oz) peeled prawns
25 g (1 oz) Gruyère cheese
100 g (4 oz) cooked white fish
2 eggs
5 tablespoons single cream
3 tablespoons milk
salt
4 drops Tabasco sauce
4 unpeeled prawns
sprigs of parsley

Roll out the pastry and line 4 individual 10 cm (4 in) flan tins. Bake blind at 200 °C/400 °F/Gas Mark 6 for 10 minutes. Trim the spring onions and chop coarsely (metal blade). Melt the butter in a pan and cook the onions for 2 minutes, stirring well. Stir the peeled prawns into the butter. Put the onion and prawn mixture into the base of the flans. Grate the cheese (disc A) and keep on one side. Break the fish into pieces and put into the processor bowl. Add the eggs, cream and milk and mix (plastic blade) until the fish is broken up into small pieces. Add the cheese, salt and Tabasco sauce. Pour into the pastry cases. Bake at 180 °C/350 °F/Gas Mark 4 for 30 minutes. Garnish with unpeeled prawns and sprigs of parsley. Serve very hot.

# Individual Cheese Soufflés

100 g (4 oz) Cheddar cheese
50 g (2 oz) shelled prawns
25 g (1 oz) Parmesan cheese
150 ml (¼ pint) milk
25 g (1 oz) plain flour
25 g (1 oz) butter
salt and pepper
4 eggs, separated
pinch of paprika pepper

Grate the Cheddar cheese (disc A). Chop the prawns finely (metal blade). Grate the Parmesan cheese (disc A). Keep both cheeses and prawns on one side. Put the milk and flour into the bowl and mix well (plastic blade). Melt the butter in a heavy-based pan and stir in the milk mixture. Season well and stir until the mixture comes to the boil. Cook for 2 minutes. Cool slightly and return to the processor bowl with the egg yolks and Cheddar cheese. Mix until smooth, turn into another bowl and stir in the prawns. Whisk the egg whites to stiff peaks (whisk attachment) and fold into the mixture. Grease 4–6 individual soufflé dishes and divide the mixture between them. Sprinkle with Parmesan cheese. Put on a baking sheet and bake at 190 °C/375 °F/Gas Mark 5 for 25 minutes. Sprinkle with paprika and serve at once.

# Bacon and Herb Puffs

Grate the cheese (disc A) and keep on one side. Put the butter and water into a pan and bring to the boil. Tip in the flour and cook gently, stirring well, for 2 minutes. Cool for 10 minutes, then put into the bowl (plastic blade). With machine running, add the eggs one at a time through the feeder tube, mixing until completely incorporated. Grease 4–6 individual soufflé dishes. Put the mixture into a piping bag fitted with a large plain nozzle and pipe round the inside of the soufflé dishes. Put on to a baking sheet and bake at 220 °C/425 °F/Gas Mark 7 for 20 minutes.

   Meanwhile, prepare the filling. Peel the onion and derind the bacon. Chop roughly together (metal blade). Wipe the mushrooms and chop (metal blade). Melt the butter in a pan and cook the onion, bacon and mushroom over low heat, stirring well, for 5 minutes. Stir in the flour and cook for 1 minute, then add the milk and continue stirring over low heat for 5 minutes. Stir in the herbs and season to taste with salt and pepper. Take the soufflé dishes from the oven and spoon the bacon mixture into the centre of each puff. Sprinkle with the grated cheese and return to the oven for 7 minutes. Serve very hot.

50 g (2 oz) Cheddar cheese
50 g (2 oz) butter
150 ml ($\frac{1}{4}$ pint) water
65 g (2$\frac{1}{2}$ oz) plain flour
2 eggs

*Filling*
1 small onion
100 g (4 oz) bacon
50 g (2 oz) mushrooms
50 g (2 oz) butter
40 g (1$\frac{1}{2}$ oz) plain flour
300 ml ($\frac{1}{2}$ pint) milk
1 tablespoon chopped fresh
   herbs
salt and pepper

# Crab Mousse

If fresh crabmeat is not available use a pack of frozen brown and white crabmeat. Make up the aspic from pack crystals and leave until cool and just setting. Grate the rind from the lemon and squeeze out the juice (juice extractor). Grate the cheese (disc A). Chop the crabmeat finely (metal blade). Add the aspic jelly, egg yolks, sherry, lemon rind and juice, cheese, ketchup and Tabasco sauce. Continue processing until smooth and creamy. Tip into a bowl and leave until just beginning to set. Whisk the egg whites until very stiff (whisk attachment) and fold into the mixture. Put into a serving dish. Chill for 2 hours. Cut the hard-boiled eggs into pieces and chop finely with the parsley (metal blade). Just before serving, sprinkle the egg mixture on the surface of the mousse. Serve with thin brown bread and butter.

225 g (8 oz) crabmeat
300 ml ($\frac{1}{2}$ pint) aspic
1 lemon
25 g (1 oz) Parmesan cheese
2 eggs, separated
1 tablespoon dry sherry
1 teaspoon tomato ketchup
4 drops Tabasco sauce
2 hard-boiled eggs, shelled
1 sprig of parsley

# Summer Cheese Mousse

50 g (2 oz) Cheddar cheese
300 ml (½ pint) double cream
2 eggs, separated
1 teaspoon mustard powder
salt and pepper
pinch of ground nutmeg

Grate the cheese (disc A) and keep on one side. Whip the cream stiffly (whisk attachment) and put into a mixing bowl. Whisk the egg yolks in a bowl over hot water until thick and creamy. Fold the egg yolks, cheese and seasonings into the whipped cream. Whisk the egg whites to stiff peaks (whisk attachment) and fold into the mixture. Fill 4–6 individual dishes and chill for an hour before serving with fingers of hot toast, or thin brown bread and butter.

# Jellied Parsley Ham

1 kg (2 lb) middle gammon
1 beef bone
3 pig's trotters
1 onion
2 bay leaves
3 sprigs of tarragon
1 sprig of thyme
large bunch of parsley
1 bottle dry white wine
1 egg white plus egg shell
1 tablespoon white wine
   vinegar

Soak the gammon in cold water for 3 hours and drain well. Meanwhile, put the beef bone, trotters, onion, bay leaves, tarragon, thyme and 1 parsley sprig into a pan. Reserve 150 ml (¼ pint) wine and pour the rest into the pan, adding a little water if necessary to cover the bones. Bring to the boil, cover and then simmer for 3 hours. Add the gammon and continue simmering for 1¼ hours until the ham is tender. Lift out the gammon and cut into pieces. Chop lean and fat coarsely (metal blade) and press lightly into a glass bowl. Strain the stock through a fine sieve and leave until cold. Remove all fat from the surface. Heat the stock until it melts completely. Whisk the egg white lightly (whisk attachment). Wash the egg shell and crush into small pieces. Add to the stock with the egg white. Bring gently to the boil and boil hard for 2 minutes, whisking to make the stock foamy. Remove from the heat, cover and leave to stand for 15 minutes. Strain through some filter paper or 3 thicknesses of kitchen paper in a sieve. Pour a little of this clear stock over the ham to moisten it. Chill the remaining stock in the refrigerator and when it is just setting, stir in the reserved wine and wine vinegar. Chop the remaining parsley finely (metal blade) and stir into the stock. Pour over the ham and leave to set. The finished dish consists of small tender pieces of pink and white ham in a beautiful green jelly. It makes a delicious first course, or is suitable for a main meal with salad.

# Chicken and Ham Spread

Cut the chicken and ham into small pieces, being sure to include the ham fat. Peel the onion and cut into small pieces. Wash, trim and cut the celery. Chop the chicken, ham, onion and celery finely (metal blade). Add the mayonnaise, chutney, vinegar, salt and pepper and continue processing until smooth. Cut the eggs into pieces and add to the mixture. Process until the eggs are finely chopped. Put into a serving dish and keep in the refrigerator to use with toast or in sandwiches.

175 g (6 oz) cooked chicken
100 g (4 oz) cooked ham
1 small onion
1 celery stick
4 tablespoons mayonnaise
2 tablespoons sweet chutney
½ teaspoon vinegar
salt and pepper
2 hard-boiled eggs, shelled

# Beef and Bacon Spread

Cut the beef and bacon into small pieces and chop finely (metal blade). Soften the butter slightly but do not melt. Add butter, mustard, Worcestershire sauce, pepper and garlic salt to the meat. Continue processing until smooth and creamy. Put into a serving dish and keep in the refrigerator to use with toast or in sandwiches.

175 g (6 oz) rare-cooked beef
50 g (2 oz) cooked bacon
50 g (2 oz) butter
1 teaspoon French mustard
1 teaspoon Worcestershire
    sauce
pepper
garlic salt

# Peanut Butter

Chop the peanuts finely (metal blade). Add the oil and continue processing until smooth. Store in a screwtop jar. For a very fresh flavour, buy peanuts in the shell, roast them in the oven and then shell them. Use them with their skins on and salt to taste.

225 g (8 oz) salted peanuts
3 tablespoons salad oil

*Crunchy Peanut Butter*
Chop peanuts coarsely (metal blade). Remove one-third of the nuts and keep on one side. Continue chopping until the nuts are very fine, then add oil and process until smooth. Stir in the remaining nuts before putting into a storage jar.

*Peanut Honey Butter*
Process basic peanut butter, adding 2 tablespoons of clear honey.

# Aubergine Caviar

2 aubergines
2 thin-skinned lemons
2 garlic cloves
100 ml (4 fl oz) salad oil
½ teaspoon salt

Trim the stem and base from each aubergine. Split them through lengthways and place cut-side down on an ungreased baking sheet. Bake at 200 °C/400 °F/Gas Mark 6 for 45 minutes. Cool completely and then scrape the flesh out of the skins. Cut the lemons in quarters and discard the pips. Cut each piece of lemon in half and half again. Chop the lemon pieces (including skin) very finely (metal blade). Peel the garlic and add to the processor with the aubergine flesh, oil, and salt and continue mixing until smooth. Put into a serving bowl and chill for 2 hours before serving with pieces of raw vegetables or salted cocktail biscuits.

# Soft Cheese Dips

175 g (6 oz) full fat soft cheese
3 tablespoons single cream
salt and pepper

Cut the cheese into small pieces. Mix with the cream, salt and pepper to a soft dipping consistency (plastic blade). This makes the basic dip which can then be flavoured (see below). Add flavouring ingredients (metal blade) and chop them finely into the dip mixture. Serve with small cocktail biscuits, crisps or pieces of raw vegetables.

*Salad Dip*
Add 1 small green pepper, 3 spring onions, ½ unpeeled cucumber, 1 garlic clove, sprig of parsley, sprig of thyme.

*Pickle Dip*
Add 100 g (4 oz) salted cocktail nuts, 1 tablespoon sweet pickle, 6 cocktail onions.

*Devil Dip*
Add 2 hard-boiled eggs, 1 small onion, 2 tablespoons mustard pickle, 2 tablespoons vinegar, 1 teaspoon curry powder.

*Horseradish Dip*
Add 1 small onion, 2 tablespoons horseradish cream, 2 rashers grilled lean bacon, 1 tablespoon mayonnaise.

*Autumn Dip*
Add 1 red-skinned eating apple (with peel on), 2 celery sticks, 50 g (2 oz) walnut halves.

# Hot Cheese Dip

Cut the cheese into small pieces and then chop finely (metal blade). Keep on one side. Mix the milk, flour and curry powder until well blended (blender attachment). Put the butter into a heavy-based pan and melt. Pour in the milk mixture and cook over moderate heat, stirring well until the mixture boils. Simmer for 3 minutes, then stir in the cheese over very low heat until the cheese has just melted. Remove from the heat and stir in the tomato purée, salt and pepper to taste. Keep warm on a hot plate and use for dipping crisps or bread cubes.

225 g (8 oz) Gruyère or
  Cheddar cheese
600 ml (1 pint) milk
50 g (2 oz) plain flour
½ teaspoon curry powder
50 g (2 oz) butter
2 teaspoons tomato purée
salt and pepper

# Italian Hot Garlic Dip

Peel the garlic and cut into small pieces. Cut each anchovy into pieces. Remove stem and seeds from peppers and cut the flesh into small pieces. Put into the bowl with the olive oil and chop very finely (metal blade). Melt the butter and, with the machine running, pour it into the feeder tube until the mixture is creamy. Put into a pan with the lemon juice and pepper to taste. Heat very slowly until the mixture boils and then simmer for 10 minutes until creamy. Keep hot over a table heater or hotplate. Serve with crusty bread and a selection of raw vegetables for dipping. This hot dip is particularly good with summer vegetables such as radishes, tiny tomatoes, cauliflower sprigs, spring onions, fennel and crisp lettuce hearts.

5 garlic cloves
8 anchovy fillets
2 red peppers
150 ml (¼ pint) olive oil
150 g (5 oz) butter
1 teaspoon lemon juice
pepper

# Tuna Olive Dip

Remove green tops from onions and trim root ends. Put into the bowl with the olives, drained tuna fish, mayonnaise and lemon juice. Process until the onions and olives are very finely chopped (metal blade). Season to taste with pepper. Chill for an hour before serving with Italian bread sticks or small cocktail biscuits.

2 spring onions
12 black olives, stoned
200 g (7 oz) canned tuna fish
4 tablespoons mayonnaise
1 tablespoon lemon juice
pepper

# Prawn Dip

225 g (8 oz) shelled prawns
100 g (4 oz) crabmeat
225 g (8 oz) full fat soft cheese
150 ml ($\frac{1}{4}$ pint) natural yogurt
1 tablespoon tomato ketchup
1 tablespoon lemon juice
salt and pepper

Chop the prawns coarsely (metal blade). Keep on one side. Put all the other ingredients into the bowl and mix thoroughly until smooth and creamy (plastic blade). Add to the prawns and stir just enough to distribute the prawns. Chill for an hour before serving with small salted biscuits.

# Blue Cheese Dip

1 small carrot
1 onion
225 g (8 oz) cottage cheese
100 g (4 oz) Danish Blue
    cheese
3 tablespoons soured cream
3 sprigs of parsley
1 garlic clove
salt and pepper
4 drops Tabasco sauce

Peel the carrot and onion and cut into pieces. Chop finely (metal blade). Add the cottage cheese and the Danish Blue cheese broken into small pieces, and process. Add the soured cream, parsley, garlic, salt, pepper and Tabasco sauce. Continue mixing until smooth. Adjust seasoning and put into serving bowl. Chill for an hour before serving with crisps or pieces of raw vegetables.

# 5. Pâtés

Pâtés are very quickly and easily made with a food processor, as the metal blade will chop raw or cooked meat, poultry or fish to either a coarse or a very fine texture. A terrine is the dish in which pâtés are cooked, but the name is often given to coarse-cut pâté; or to one in which there are alternate layers of finely processed ingredients and large pieces; or layers of the main pâté are alternated with a vegetable layer.

A pâté should be carefully flavoured with herbs and alcohol and seasoning, and it is a good idea to make a 'seasoning' test before cooking the pâté. To do this, take a spoonful of the finished mixture and cook it quickly in butter over high heat. Taste the pâté and adjust the seasoning of the mixture before putting it into the container for cooking. If a pâté is prepared in an earthenware oven dish, the dish may be taken to the table, but if it has to be made in a loaf tin, the pâté must of course be turned on to a serving dish.

The container should be placed in an oven roasting tin containing water, as this will mean that the pâté is cooked in a low moist heat and will not dry out. It is cooked when it has shrunk slightly from the sides of the container and when a knitting needle or sharp knife comes out clean. Juices which run out should be clear, not pink, but the meat should still retain a slightly pink tinge, rather than grey.

When the pâté is cooked, cover with foil and then place weights on top, or tins of food. Leave for at least 6 hours in a cold place so that it will be firm enough to cut neatly, but the pâté will be at its best if left for 24 hours when the flavours will have blended and matured.

# Seafood Pâté

450 g (1 lb) fresh prawns or
    shrimps
450 g (1 lb) haddock
50 g (2 oz) butter
1 teaspoon anchovy essence
pinch of ground mace
pinch of cayenne pepper
100 g (4 oz) clarified butter

Shell the prawns or shrimps and put the shells into a sauce-pan. Add just enough liquid to cover and bring to the boil. Strain the liquid and put into a saucepan. Discard the shells. Cut the haddock in pieces and add to the liquid. Simmer for 10 minutes until the haddock is tender. Chop the prawns or shrimps coarsely (metal blade) and put into a bowl. Drain the haddock and break into large flakes. Put into the processor bowl with slightly softened butter, anchovy essence, mace and cayenne pepper. Mix thoroughly (plastic blade) until smooth. Add to the prawns or shrimps and stir them in until well mixed (the creamy fish mixture should be stuffed with large pieces of pink shellfish). Put into a serving dish. Chill for 1 hour. Melt the clarified butter and pour over chilled mixture. Chill for an hour before serving with toast.

# Taramasalata

225 g (8 oz) smoked cod's roe
2 thin slices white bread (large
    loaf)
2 tablespoons milk
2 garlic cloves
150 ml ($\frac{1}{4}$ pint) olive oil
2 tablespoons lemon juice
pepper
2 tablespoons double cream or
    natural yogurt

The cod's roe may be fresh or from a jar. If fresh, remove the skin before processing. Discard crusts from the bread and soak the bread in the milk for 10 minutes. Peel the garlic and mix with the cod's roe and soaked bread until very smooth (metal blade). With the machine running, pour the oil slowly through the feeder tube until the mixture looks like mayonnaise (metal blade). Add the lemon juice, pepper, cream or yogurt and mix until just combined (plastic blade). Place in a serving dish and chill for an hour before serving with toast.

# Smoked Salmon Pâté

450 g (1 lb) smoked salmon
50 g (2 oz) unsalted butter
1 tablespoon lemon juice
1 tablespoon dry sherry
pinch of pepper
150 ml ($\frac{1}{4}$ pint) double cream

Smoked salmon trimmings may sometimes be bought for preparing this pâté. Chop finely (metal blade). Soften the butter slightly, but do not let it melt. Add to the salmon with the lemon juice, sherry and pepper. Mix until just smooth (plastic blade). Add the cream and mix again until light and creamy. Put into a serving dish and chill for an hour before serving with toast or on canapés.

# Sardine Pâté

Mix the sardines and oil until broken up (plastic blade). Add the cheese cut into pieces, with the lemon juice, salt, pepper and cayenne pepper. Continue mixing until well blended. Cut the eggs in pieces and put into the bowl. Mix long enough for the eggs to be finely chopped. Put into a serving dish and chill for an hour before serving. Serve with toast or in sandwiches.

90 g (3½ oz) canned sardines in oil
150 g (5 oz) full fat soft cheese
1 tablespoon lemon juice
salt and pepper
pinch of cayenne pepper
2 hard-boiled eggs, shelled

# Rich Pork Terrine

Cut the lean and fat pork and the liver into 2·5 cm (1 in) pieces. Peel the onion and cut it into pieces. Peel the garlic. Chop the meat, onion and garlic finely (metal blade) and turn into a bowl. Discard the crusts and break the bread in small pieces. Make into crumbs (metal blade). Blend all the ingredients until smooth (blender attachment). Press the mixture into an ovenware container and cover with a lid or piece of foil. Stand the container in a roasting tin with hot water to come half-way up the dish. Cook at 170 °C/325 °F/Gas Mark 3 for 2 hours. Remove the lid. Cover the pâté with foil and put weights on top. Leave for 24 hours before serving in slices with salad or toast.

350 g (12 oz) lean pork
100 g (4 oz) fat pork
100 g (4 oz) pig's liver
1 small onion
1 garlic clove
50 g (2 oz) day-old white bread
1 egg
4 sage leaves
1 teaspoon fresh rosemary
salt and pepper
pinch of ground nutmeg
1 tablespoon brandy or dry sherry

# Chicken Liver Pâté

Cut the livers into pieces and chop finely (metal blade). Keep on one side. Peel the onion. Cut the bacon and onion into pieces and chop finely (metal blade). Melt the butter and cook the onion and bacon gently for 5 minutes. Peel the garlic cloves. Put the livers, onion, bacon, butter juices, garlic, egg, salt and pepper into the bowl and process until smooth (plastic blade). Put into an ovenware container, and cover with a lid or foil. Stand the container in a roasting tin with hot water to come half-way up the dish. Cook at 180 °C/350 °F/ Gas Mark 4 for 1 hour. Remove the lid. Cover the pâté with foil and put weights on top. Leave for 4 hours until cold. Melt the clarified butter and pour over the surface to cover the pâté completely. Leave until the butter has set firmly. Serve with toast.

225 g (8 oz) chicken livers
1 small onion
75 g (3 oz) fat bacon
25 g (1 oz) butter
2 garlic cloves
1 egg
salt and pepper
50 g (2 oz) clarified butter

1. Chopping pork and bacon

2. Adding onion and garlic

3. Chopping spinach

# Pork and Spinach Pâté

1 bay leaf
225 g (8 oz) streaky bacon
   rashers
225 g (8 oz) belly of pork
100 g (4 oz) back bacon
1 small onion
½ garlic clove
1 small egg
225 g (8 oz) spinach
pepper
1 sprig of parsley
½ teaspoon fresh rosemary

Grease a 450 g (1 lb) loaf tin or terrine and put the bay leaf in it. Remove the rind from the bacon and spread the rashers out thinly with a palette knife. Use two-thirds of the rashers to line the terrine. Cut the pork and back bacon into small pieces and chop finely (metal blade). Peel the onion and garlic, cut into pieces and add them to the meat. Process until finely chopped. Take out half the mixture and keep on one side. Add the parsley, rosemary and egg to the bowl and process until the mixture is creamy. Keep on one side. Wash the spinach and put into a saucepan. Cover and cook over high heat (do not add any water) for 4–5 minutes until just tender. Drain off surplus liquid. Put into the mixer bowl and chop finely but do not mix to a purée (metal blade). Mix the spinach with the two meat mixtures and season well with pepper. Put into the lined dish and cover with remaining bacon rashers. Cover with a piece of foil and a lid and put the dish into a roasting tin with hot water to come half-way up the dish. Cook at 170 °C/325 °F/Gas Mark 3 for 1½ hours. Remove from the roasting tin. Remove the lid and put weights on the foil. Leave for 24 hours before turning out of the dish. Serve in thick slices with salad.

# Bacon Pâté

350 g (12 oz) unsmoked bacon
   rashers
450 g (1 lb) lean pork
1 small onion
175 g (6 oz) day-old white
   bread
2 eggs
2 hard-boiled eggs, shelled
salt and pepper
pinch of ground nutmeg
pinch of dried mixed herbs

Derind the bacon and smooth out 6 rashers with a palette knife. Line a 1 kg (2 lb) terrine, casserole or loaf tin with them. Cut the remaining bacon into small pieces. Cut the pork into 2·5 cm (1 in) pieces. Peel the onion and cut it into eighths. Chop the bacon, pork and onion together finely (metal blade) and tip into a bowl. Discard crusts and break the bread into pieces. Make into crumbs (metal blade). Put into the bowl with the meat and add the eggs. Chop the hard-boiled eggs coarsely (metal blade) and add to the meat. Season with salt, pepper, nutmeg and herbs and stir until well mixed. Put the meat mixture into the container and cover with a lid or piece of foil. Place the container in a roasting tin with hot water to come half-way up the dish. Cook at 180 °C/350 °F/Gas Mark 4 for 1¼ hours. Remove the lid. Cover the pâté with foil and put weights on top. Leave for 24 hours before turning out of the container. Serve with salad, or toast, or use for sandwiches.

# Turkey Terrine

350 g (12 oz) cooked turkey
2 tablespoons brandy
225 g (8 oz) fat pork
1 onion
25 g (1 oz) butter
100 g (4 oz) white bread
4 tablespoons milk
1 egg
salt and pepper
pinch of ground nutmeg
pinch of dried mixed herbs

This is an excellent way of using leftover Christmas turkey but the terrine can of course be made with an individual turkey joint or rolled turkey now available. Use a mixture of dark and light meat from the turkey. Cut the meat into small pieces and chop coarsely (metal blade). Put into a bowl with the brandy and leave to stand while processing other ingredients. Cut the pork into small pieces and chop finely (metal blade). Keep on one side. Peel the onion, cut into quarters and chop finely (metal blade). Heat the butter and cook the onion until soft and golden. Mix the onion and butter with the pork. Soak the bread in the milk for 10 minutes and thoroughly mix with the pork, onion, butter, egg, salt, pepper, nutmeg and herbs (plastic blade). Thoroughly grease an ovenware container. Put half the mixture in it and top with turkey pieces, sprinkling with brandy. Cover with the remaining mixture. Cover with a lid or piece of foil. Stand the container in a roasting tin with hot water to come half-way up the dish. Cook at 180 °C/350 °F/Gas Mark 4 for 1¼ hours. Remove the lid. Cover the pâté with foil and put weights on top. Leave for 24 hours before serving in slices with a salad.

# Game Terrine

Try to have a mixture of light and dark meat, and if little light meat is available add a chicken joint to the game. Pheasant, pigeon, hare and rabbit are all good in a mixed game pâté. Remove skin from the game and cut the flesh in small pieces. Cut the bacon into pieces. Cut them both coarsely in the bowl (metal blade) and tip into a basin with the brandy. Leave to stand for 1 hour. Cut the pork into small pieces and then chop very finely (metal blade). Mix with the game, bacon and brandy. Season well with salt, pepper, nutmeg and herbs and stir in the egg until well blended. Put into an ovenware container and cover with a lid or foil. Stand the container in a roasting tin with hot water to come half-way up the dish. Cook at 180°C/350°F/Gas Mark 4 for 1½ hours. Remove the lid. Cover the pâté with foil and put weights on top. Leave for 24 hours before serving in slices with salad or toast.

675 g (1½ lb) mixed uncooked game
100 g (4 oz) fat bacon
3 tablespoons brandy
350 g (12 oz) lean pork
salt and pepper
pinch of ground nutmeg
pinch of dried mixed herbs
1 egg

# Potted Beef

Peel the onion and cut it into eighths. Chop finely (metal blade). Put into a casserole. Cut the steak into cubes and add to the casserole with the mace, allspice, salt, pepper, parsley, thyme, bay leaf and stock. Cover and cook at 150°C/300°F/Gas Mark 2 for 2½ hours. Leave the meat to cool in the stock. Drain the meat, reserving the stock. Discard the herbs. Put the meat into the bowl with 2 tablespoons stock, butter, port or sherry and anchovy essence. Mix until completely smooth (metal blade). Spoon into a serving dish and chill for an hour before serving with toast, or as a sandwich filling.

1 small onion
450 g (1 lb) chuck steak
pinch of ground mace
pinch of ground allspice
salt and pepper
1 sprig of parsley
1 sprig of thyme
1 bay leaf
150 ml (¼ pint) beef stock
50 g (2 oz) butter
1 tablespoon port or sherry
¼ teaspoon anchovy essence

# 6. Main Courses

There need be no excuse for inadequate meals which lack nourishment when a food processor can prepare fresh ingredients in less time than it takes to deal with convenience food. A food processor can chop fresh or cooked meat, make pastry or suet crusts, and whip up smooth sauces. While the main dish is cooking, vegetables or salads can be chopped, grated, sliced or shredded, or potato chips quickly made. The swift preparation of breadcrumbs, grated cheese or savoury butters will give a professional finish to the most basic fish and meat dishes.

If chopping raw meat, trim off any fat, skin or gristle, and cut into 2·5 cm (1 in) cubes. Put 175–225 g (6–8 oz) meat into the bowl and process for about 5 seconds. The meat may be chopped coarsely, or almost reduced to a paste, according to the length of time the machine is running. Meat may be seasoned before chopping, but flavourings intensify during processing, so do not over-season at first, as adjustments can easily be made during cooking.

If chopping cooked meat, follow the same method as for raw meat. About 3 seconds will give the right consistency for minced meat dishes such as shepherd's pie. Other ingredients such as onions or carrots may be added during the chopping process, and liquids or eggs can be added through the feeder tube while the machine is running.

# Stuffed Plaice in Shrimp Sauce

Skin the fish and make a cut down the centre of one side of each fish. Peel the onion and chop finely (metal blade). Wipe the mushrooms. Melt the butter and cook the onion and mushrooms gently, stirring well, for 5 minutes. Discard the crusts from the bread and make bread into fine crumbs (metal blade). Add the onion mixture to the crumbs and season well. Insert this stuffing into the cuts in the fish. Grease an ovenware dish and place the fish in it. Bake at 200°C/400°F/Gas Mark 6 for 20 minutes.

Make the sauce by blending the butter, flour and milk (blender attachment). Heat and stir over low heat until the sauce is thick and creamy. Grate the lemon rind and keep on one side. Squeeze out the juice (juice extractor) and add to the sauce. Season to taste. Chop the shrimps or prawns coarsely (metal blade). Add to the sauce and heat through. Pour over the fish and continue baking for 15 minutes. Chop the parsley finely (metal blade) and mix with the grated lemon rind. Just before serving, sprinkle the parsley and lemon on to the fish.

4 small plaice
1 small onion
50 g (2 oz) button mushrooms
25 g (1 oz) butter
75 g (3 oz) day-old white bread
salt and pepper

*Sauce*
25 g (1 oz) butter
25 g (1 oz) plain flour
450 ml (¾ pint) milk
1 lemon
salt and pepper
100 g (4 oz) peeled shrimps or
   prawns
1 sprig of parsley

# Plaice Florentine

Wash the spinach thoroughly and remove the stems. Put into a pan without additional water. Cover and cook gently for 3 minutes, shaking the pan frequently. Cool slightly and put into the processor bowl. Add half the butter and the cream and process to make a purée (metal blade). Season well. Thoroughly grease an ovenware dish and put the purée in it. Put the plaice fillets on top. Discard the crusts from the bread and make bread into fine crumbs (metal blade). Grate the cheese (disc A). Mix the crumbs and cheese and season lightly. Sprinkle on top of the fish and dot with flakes of the remaining butter. Bake at 200°C/400°F/Gas Mark 6 for 20 minutes.

450 g (1 lb) spinach
50 g (2 oz) butter
4 tablespoons single cream
salt and pepper
4 plaice fillets
50 g (2 oz) day-old white bread
25 g (1 oz) Cheddar cheese

# Portuguese Cod

4 cod steaks
100 g (4 oz) streaky bacon
1 large onion
1 green pepper
1 tablespoon oil
450 g (1 lb) canned tomatoes
1 tablespoon tomato purée
½ teaspoon dried mixed herbs
salt and pepper
1 large sprig of parsley

Grease an ovenware dish. Grill the cod steaks and put them in it. Derind the bacon and chop coarsely (metal blade). Peel the onion and chop finely (metal blade). Remove the stem and seeds from the pepper and chop coarsely (metal blade). Heat the oil in a pan and cook the bacon, onion and pepper for 5 minutes until soft and golden. Add the tomatoes and their juice, tomato purée, herbs, salt and pepper. Cover and simmer for 10 minutes. Pour over the cod and bake at 170 °C/325 °F/Gas Mark 3 for 20 minutes. Chop the parsley finely (metal blade) and sprinkle on top just before serving.

# Savoury Baked Trout

4 × 225 g (8 oz) trout
1 small onion
3 sage leaves
75 g (3 oz) butter
50 g (2 oz) day-old white bread
salt and pepper
225 g (8 oz) button mushrooms
150 ml (¼ pint) single cream

Grease an ovenware dish. Clean and gut the trout and remove heads and tails. Put into the dish, cover with a piece of greased greaseproof paper and bake at 180 °C/350 °F/Gas Mark 4 for 20 minutes. Meanwhile, peel the onion and with the sage leaves chop finely (metal blade). Melt half the butter in a pan and cook the onion for 5 minutes over low heat until soft. Discard the crusts from the bread, make the bread into crumbs (metal blade) and stir into the onions. Season well and remove from the heat. Wipe the mushrooms and chop coarsely (metal blade). Cook in the remaining butter over low heat for 5 minutes, stirring well. Stir in the cream and heat for 1 minute. Pour the mushrooms and cream over the baked trout. Sprinkle with the breadcrumb mixture and bake for 10 minutes. Serve very hot with boiled potatoes and peas or beans.

# Stuffed Trout in Jackets

Roll out the pastry to a large square and cut into 4 lengths slightly shorter than the trout. Skin the trout, remove backbone but leave the heads and tails in place. Peel the onion and chop finely (metal blade). Melt the butter in a pan and cook the onion for 5 minutes over low heat until soft. Wipe the mushrooms and chop finely (metal blade). Add to the onions and cook for 3 minutes. Chop the watercress finely (metal blade) and stir into the onion mixture. Discard the crusts from the bread and make bread into crumbs (metal blade). Add the breadcrumbs to the onion mixture with the lemon rind, salt and pepper. Fill the trout with this stuffing. Put a trout on to each piece of pastry and fold over to enclose each fish, leaving head and tail showing. Seal edges well and brush over with beaten egg. Put on to a baking sheet and bake at 200 °C/400 °F/Gas Mark 6 for 30 minutes. Serve hot or cold.

450 g (1 lb) made shortcrust
   pastry (page 86)
4 × 225 g (8 oz) trout
1 onion
25 g (1 oz) butter
50 g (2 oz) button mushrooms
1 bunch watercress
75 g (3 oz) day-old white bread
½ teaspoon grated lemon rind
salt and pepper
beaten egg for glazing

# Beef and Walnut Roll

Mix the flour, salt, suet, herbs and water to a soft dough (plastic blade). Place on a floured surface and roll into a rectangle 28 × 33 cm (11 × 13 in). Cut the steak into pieces and chop finely (metal blade). Peel the onion and chop the onion and walnuts finely (metal blade). Mix with the meat. Discard the crusts from the bread and make bread into crumbs (metal blade). Fry the meat mixture in the oil, stirring well for 5 minutes. Drain off surplus oil. Mix the breadcrumbs and chutney into the meat mixture and spread on the pastry to within 1 cm (½ in) of the edge. Roll up like a Swiss roll and pinch the edges to seal. Grease a piece of foil and put the roll on it with the seam underneath. Fold over the foil loosely, and place on a baking sheet. Bake at 180 °C/350 °F/Gas Mark 4 for 1 hour. Remove the foil and continue baking for 15 minutes. Serve in thick slices with gravy.

200 g (7 oz) self-raising flour
pinch of salt
100 g (4 oz) shredded suet
pinch of dried mixed herbs
4–5 tablespoons cold water
450 g (1 lb) chuck steak
1 small onion
50 g (2 oz) walnut halves
50 g (2 oz) day-old white bread
1 tablespoon oil
3 tablespoons chutney

# Spicy Spanish Loaf

2 tomatoes
450 g (1 lb) chuck steak
1 red pepper
1 garlic clove
75 g (3 oz) day-old white bread
50 g (2 oz) tomato purée
1 teaspoon chopped fresh basil
   or marjoram
1 teaspoon Tabasco sauce
1 egg
salt and pepper
8 Spanish stuffed olives

Grease a 450 g (1 lb) loaf tin. Wipe the tomatoes, slice cross-ways and arrange in base of the tin. Cut the steak into pieces and chop finely (metal blade). Remove stem and seeds from the pepper and peel the garlic. Chop the pepper and garlic together finely (metal blade) and mix with the meat. Discard the crusts from the bread and make bread into crumbs (metal blade). Mix into the meat with the tomato purée, basil or marjoram, Tabasco sauce, egg, salt and pepper. Put into the loaf tin, cover with foil and bake at 170 °C/325 °F/Gas Mark 3 for 1½ hours. Remove the foil and turn on to a serving dish. Garnish with thinly sliced olives.

# Spanish Peppers

350 g (12 oz) chuck steak
1 carrot
1 onion
12 Spanish stuffed olives
1 tablespoon tomato purée
salt and pepper
4 green peppers
400 g (14 oz) canned tomatoes

Cut the steak in pieces and chop finely (metal blade). Peel the carrot and onion. Chop the carrot, onion and olives finely together (metal blade). Mix the steak, carrot, onion and olives with the tomato purée, salt and pepper. Remove stems and seeds from the peppers. Put into a pan, cover with cold water and bring to the boil. Simmer for 5 minutes, then drain off the water. Grease an ovenware dish, stand the peppers in it and fill them with the meat mixture. Blend the tomatoes and their juice (blender attachment). Put through a sieve to get rid of the pips. Season well and pour over the peppers. Cover the dish with a piece of foil and bake at 190 °C/375 °F/Gas Mark 5 for 45 minutes. Remove the foil, spoon the liquid over the peppers, and continue baking for 15 minutes. Serve with boiled rice.

# Savoury Meat Loaf

350 g (12 oz) chuck steak
350 g (12 oz) lean pork
300 g (10 oz) day-old white
   bread
1 garlic clove
25 g (1 oz) parsley
2 eggs
2 tablespoons tomato purée
1 teaspoon salt
1 teaspoon black pepper

Cut the steak and pork into pieces and chop them finely (metal blade). Discard the crusts from the bread and make bread into crumbs (metal blade). Peel the garlic and chop with the parsley (metal blade). Mix all the ingredients together. Put into a loaf tin and cover with a piece of foil. Put the loaf tin into a roasting tin and pour in water so that it comes 2·5 cm (1 in) up the loaf tin. Cook at 170 °C/325 °F/Gas Mark 3 for 2 hours. Serve hot with gravy or tomato sauce and vegetables, or cold with salad or in sandwiches.

# Beef Croquettes

Cut the beef into pieces and chop finely (metal blade). Discard crusts from day-old bread and make bread into crumbs (metal blade). Chop the cucumber (metal blade). Blend the flour and milk together (plastic blade). Melt the butter in a pan and stir in the milk mixture. Cook over low heat, stirring well, until thick and creamy. Mix in the meat, bread, cucumber, herbs, salt and pepper. Leave until cold and then form into 8 sausage shapes. Break the hard bread into pieces and make into breadcrumbs (metal blade). Beat the egg lightly with a fork and coat each croquette with egg, then coat with breadcrumbs. Fry in hot oil until crisp and brown. Serve hot with vegetables or cold with salad.

350 g (12 oz) cooked beef
100 g (4 oz) day-old white bread
25 g (1 oz) pickled cucumber
25 g (1 oz) plain flour
150 ml (¼ pint) milk
25 g (1 oz) butter
2 teaspoons chopped fresh herbs
salt and pepper
50 g (2 oz) hard bread
1 egg
oil for deep frying

# Peppered Beefburgers in Wine Sauce

Cut the steak into pieces and chop finely (metal blade). Peel the onion and chop finely (metal blade). Mix the steak and onion together and season well. Form into 4 balls and then flatten slightly. Grind the peppercorns in a peppermill and press the pepper into both sides of the meat. Heat the oil and butter together in a frying pan and fry the meat on both sides on medium heat for 10 minutes, turning once. Drain off surplus fat. Add the wine to the pan and scrape the pan drippings with a spoon to mix with the wine. Add the herbs and simmer for 5 minutes. Serve with vegetables or a salad and crusty bread. For the flavour of this dish, it is most important that freshly-ground pepper and fresh herbs are used.

450 g (1 lb) rump steak
1 onion
salt and pepper
1 tablespoon black peppercorns
1 tablespoon oil
25 g (1 oz) butter
150 ml (¼ pint) red wine
1 teaspoon chopped fresh herbs

# Savoury Meatballs with Barbecue Sauce

350 g (12 oz) chuck steak
1 onion
8 sage leaves
50 g (2 oz) day-old white bread
1 egg
salt and pepper
25 g (1 oz) plain flour
2 tablespoons oil

*Sauce*
2 onions
1 clove garlic
1 tablespoon oil
50 g (2 oz) tomato purée
450 g (1 lb) canned tomatoes
50 g (2 oz) dark soft brown
    sugar
2 tablespoons vinegar
½ teaspoon salt

Cut the steak into pieces and chop finely (metal blade). Peel the onion and chop finely with the sage leaves (metal blade). Discard the crusts from the bread and make bread into crumbs (metal blade). Mix together the meat, onion, crumbs and egg and season with salt and pepper. Shape into 16 balls and roll them lightly in the flour. Heat the oil in a pan and gently fry the meatballs for about 25 minutes, turning occasionally, until browned and cooked through. Drain.

Meanwhile, make the sauce. Peel the onions and slice (disc H). Peel and crush the garlic. Fry the onion and garlic in the oil for 5 minutes. Add all the other sauce ingredients and bring to the boil, stirring well. Cover and simmer for about 20 minutes until the meatballs are ready. Serve the meatballs on rice with the sauce poured over.

# Beef and Bacon Roll

450 g (1 lb) chuck steak
225 g (8 oz) streaky bacon
1 small onion
1 large carrot
100 g (4 oz) porridge oats
1 egg
1 tablespoon Worcestershire
    sauce
salt and pepper
pinch of dried mixed herbs
25 g (1 oz) browned
    breadcrumbs

Cut the steak into pieces. Derind the bacon, and cut into pieces. Chop both finely (metal blade). Peel the onion and chop finely (metal blade). Peel the carrot and grate (disc A). Mix together the steak, bacon, onion and carrot. Stir in the oats, egg, Worcestershire sauce, salt, pepper and herbs and mix well. Grease a large piece of foil. Turn the mixture on to the foil and form into a roll about 15 cm (6 in) long. Wrap in the foil and place on a baking sheet. Bake at 150°C/300°F/Gas Mark 2 for 2 hours. Leave to cool for 15 minutes before unwrapping. Press breadcrumbs all over the meat. Leave until cold. Serve in thick slices with salad or pickles.

# Minced Beef Batter

Cut the steak into pieces and chop finely (metal blade). Discard the crusts from the bread and make bread into crumbs (metal blade). Mix together the meat, bread, tomato purée, 1 egg, salt and pepper. Shape into 10 balls. Melt the lard in a roasting tin and put in the meatballs. Peel the onion and chop coarsely (metal blade). Sprinkle over the meatballs and put into the oven at 220 °C/425 °F/Gas Mark 7 for 10 minutes. Meanwhile, put the flour, salt, milk and second egg into the processor bowl and mix to a smooth batter (plastic blade). Pour over the meatballs and put in the oven at 230 °C/450 °F/Gas Mark 8 for 30 minutes. Grate the cheese (disc A). Sprinkle on to the crisp batter and return to the oven for 5 minutes. Serve at once.

225 g (8 oz) chuck steak
50 g (2 oz) day-old white bread
3 tablespoons tomato purée
2 eggs
salt and pepper
25 g (1 oz) lard
1 onion
100 g (4 oz) plain flour
pinch of salt
300 ml (½ pint) milk
50 g (2 oz) Cheddar cheese

# Beef Crumble

Cut the steak into pieces and chop finely (metal blade). Peel the onion and chop finely (metal blade). Melt the dripping and cook the meat and onion over low heat until golden brown. Add 25 g (1 oz) flour, tomato purée, stock, salt and pepper and a pinch of the herbs. Stir well and simmer for 5 minutes. Put into an ovenware dish. Put the butter and the remaining flour into the processor bowl and mix until like fine breadcrumbs (plastic blade). Grate the cheese (disc A) and mix with the flour and butter. Add the remaining mixed herbs. Sprinkle on top of the meat mixture. Bake at 190 °C/375 °F/Gas Mark 5 for 1 hour. Chop the parsley (metal blade) and sprinkle on the crumble before serving.

350 g (12 oz) chuck steak
1 large onion
25 g (1 oz) dripping
75 g (3 oz) plain flour
1 tablespoon tomato purée
300 ml (½ pint) beef stock
salt and pepper
2 teaspoons chopped fresh herbs
50 g (2 oz) butter
50 g (2 oz) Cheddar cheese
1 sprig of parsley

1. Meat and onion ready for chopping

2. Adding egg yolk, nutmeg and cream to sauce

3. Adding last layer of lasagne to dish

# Lasagne

450 g (1 lb) raw lean beef
1 small onion
1 teaspoon dried marjoram or
    sage
1 tablespoon tomato purée
300 ml (½ pint) beef stock
salt and pepper
300 g (10 oz) lasagne
75 g (3 oz) Cheddar cheese
25 g (1 oz) butter
25 g (1 oz) plain flour
300 ml (½ pint) milk
1 egg yolk
pinch of ground nutmeg
4 tablespoons single cream

Cut the meat into small pieces and peel the onion. Chop them finely (metal blade) with the marjoram or sage. Put into a pan and fry gently until the fat runs. Drain off surplus fat. Stir the purée and stock into the meat, cover and simmer for 1 hour, stirring occasionally and seasoning to taste. Cook the lasagne in boiling salted water for 10 minutes and drain well.

Grate the Cheddar cheese (disc C). Mix the butter, flour and milk for 5 minutes (plastic blade). Pour into a saucepan and bring to the boil. Reduce heat and cook for 2 minutes, stirring well. Cool for 5 minutes. Put into mixer bowl and add egg yolk, nutmeg, cream, salt and pepper. Mix for 5 seconds. Add half the cheese and mix for 5 seconds. Grease an ovenware dish and put in half the meat mixture. Cover with half the lasagne and then half the cheese sauce. Put in remaining meat and lasagne. Cover with remaining cheese sauce and sprinkle with remaining grated cheese. Bake at 180°C/350°F/Gas Mark 4 for 35 minutes until golden brown. Serve hot with a side salad.

The dish may be varied by using green (spinach) lasagne or wholemeal lasagne which will give a different colour and texture to the dish.

# Spiced Stuffed Cabbage Leaves

8 large cabbage leaves
450 g (1 lb) chuck steak
1 onion
1 sprig of parsley
1 tablespoon oil
450 g (1 lb) canned tomatoes
2 tablespoons Worcestershire
  sauce
1 tablespoon cornflour
salt and pepper

*Sauce*
1 tablespoon tomato purée
1 tablespoon cornflour
1 teaspoon Worcestershire
  sauce
½ teaspoon sugar
salt and pepper

Wash the cabbage leaves. Put into a pan of boiling water and boil for 2 minutes, then drain thoroughly. Cut the steak into pieces and chop finely (metal blade). Peel the onion and put into the processor bowl with the parsley. Chop finely (metal blade). Heat the oil in a pan and cook the onion for 5 minutes over low heat, stirring well. Add the steak and continue frying, stirring well, until lightly browned. Drain the tomatoes and reserve the liquid. Add tomatoes, Worcestershire sauce, cornflour, salt and pepper to the meat and stir well. Cover and simmer for 20 minutes, stirring occasionally. Divide the stuffing between the cabbage leaves and roll them up, folding in the edges to make neat parcels. Grease a shallow ovenware dish and put leaves into it, close together. Cover with a piece of foil and bake at 190 °C/375 °F/Gas Mark 5 for 20 minutes.

Measure the juice reserved from the tomatoes and make up to 300 ml (½ pint) with water. Blend this liquid with the sauce ingredients until smooth (blender attachment). Simmer for 3 minutes and pour over the cabbage parcels. Continue baking for 15 minutes. Serve hot with boiled rice.

# Stuffed Baked Marrow

1 marrow
2 onions
50 g (2 oz) dripping
350 g (12 oz) cooked beef
175 g (6 oz) day-old white
  bread
150 ml (¼ pint) gravy
pinch of dried sage
salt and pepper

Trim the ends from the marrow. Peel it and cut through lengthways to remove the top third of the marrow. Scoop out the seeds and pith. Peel the onions and chop them finely (metal blade). Fry in a little of the lard until soft and golden. Cut the cooked meat into pieces and then chop finely (metal blade). Stir in the onion and cook for 5 minutes. Discard the crusts from the bread, make the bread into crumbs (metal blade) and mix with the onions and the meat. Remove from the heat and stir in the gravy, sage, salt and pepper. Fill the marrow and replace the lid. Spread remaining dripping on top. Bake at 200 °C/400 °F/Gas Mark 6 for 1 hour. Serve in slices with plenty of gravy.

# Steak Tartare

Trim all fat from the steak. Cut into pieces and then chop finely (metal blade). Put into a bowl. Peel and chop the onion finely (metal blade) and add to the meat with the egg yolk, Tabasco sauce, salt and pepper. Divide the mixture into 4 portions and shape into round thick patties. Place one on each plate.

    With a soup spoon, make a depression in the centre of each patty, and put in an egg yolk. Chop the parsley finely (metal blade) and sprinkle on the meat. Chop the anchovies by hand and place a small pile next to each patty. Peel and trim the spring onions and chop finely (metal blade); arrange next to anchovies. Chop the capers by hand and arrange next to onions. Chill for 30 minutes before serving. Each person mixes the egg yolk and garnishes into the raw steak with his fork before eating.

450 g (1 lb) fillet or rump steak
1 small onion
1 egg yolk
$\frac{1}{4}$ teaspoon Tabasco sauce
salt and pepper

*Garnish*
4 egg yolks
2 large sprigs of parsley
4 anchovy fillets
4 spring onions
24 capers

# Samosas

Mix the flour, suet, salt and water to a firm dough (plastic blade). Roll out and cut into eight 7·5 cm (3 in) rounds. Cut the lamb into pieces and chop very finely (metal blade). Peel the onion and chop finely (metal blade). Heat the oil and cook the onion and curry powder for 5 minutes, stirring well. Add the lamb and continue cooking for 5 minutes. Remove from the heat and season with salt, pepper and chutney. Leave until cold. Put a spoonful of the lamb mixture into the centre of each pastry round. Pinch the edges of each round together to form a pasty shape, and seal edges firmly. Fry in deep hot oil for 5 minutes until the pastry is golden. Serve hot with chutney.

175 g (6 oz) self-raising flour
75 g (3 oz) shredded suet
pinch of salt
3–4 tablespoons cold water
175 g (6 oz) cooked lamb
1 small onion
1 tablespoon oil
1 teaspoon curry powder
salt and pepper
1 tablespoon sweet chutney
oil for deep frying

1. Chopping apricots and celery

2. Mixing apricots and celery with other stuffing ingredients

3. Tying up stuffed meat

# Roast Lamb with Apricot Stuffing

100 g (4 oz) dried apricots
225 g (8 oz) day-old white bread
2 celery sticks
50 g (2 oz) melted butter
salt and pepper
1·5 kg (3 lb) boned shoulder of lamb
3 sprigs of rosemary

Cover the apricots with water, bring to the boil and simmer for 5 minutes. Drain, reserving liquid. Discard crusts and cut the bread into pieces. Make into breadcrumbs (metal blade). Keep breadcrumbs on one side. Wash and trim celery. Cool the apricots for 10 minutes and put into the mixer bowl with pieces of celery. Chop coarsely (metal blade). Mix the apricots and celery with the reserved liquid, breadcrumbs, butter and seasoning. Stuff the lamb and tie the meat carefully so that the stuffing cannot escape. Put the joint into a roasting tin and place 1 rosemary sprig on top. Roast at 190°C/375°F/Gas Mark 5 for 2 hours, basting occasionally with pan juices. As the stuffing is richly-flavoured, the joint is best served with plainly boiled potatoes rather than roast potatoes. Before serving, replace the rosemary with fresh sprigs.

# Bakehouse Lamb

675 g (1½ lb) potatoes
225 g (8 oz) onions
salt and pepper
2 kg (4 lb) leg of lamb
4 tablespoons mint jelly
100 g (4 oz) day-old white
  bread
2 large sprigs of parsley

Peel the potatoes and slice (disc H). Peel the onions and chop coarsely (metal blade). Grease a large ovenware dish and arrange half the potatoes in a layer on the base. Season with salt and pepper. Sprinkle on the onions and then put on the remaining potatoes. Place the leg of lamb on top of this bed of vegetables. Do not add any fat as there will be enough in the lamb for roasting the meat and vegetables. Sprinkle the skin of the lamb with salt and pepper. Roast at 190 °C/375 °F/Gas Mark 5 for 1 hour. Baste the vegetables with the fat from the lamb. Spread the mint jelly on the lamb skin. Discard the crusts from the bread and put the bread into the processor bowl with the parsley. Make breadcrumbs (metal blade). Season with salt and pepper and press all over the skin of the lamb. Sprinkle a little fat on the crumbs. Continue roasting for 45 minutes. Remove the lamb to a carving dish and serve the vegetables from the ovenware dish.

# Somerset Lamb

1 kg (2 lb) boned shoulder of
  lamb
25 g (1 oz) plain flour
50 g (2 oz) butter
2 onions
1 garlic clove
2 large sprigs of parsley
150 ml (¼ pint) dry cider
150 ml (¼ pint) stock
1 tablespoon Worcestershire
  sauce
salt and pepper

Cut the meat into pieces and chop very coarsely (metal blade). Coat the meat with the flour and fry in the butter until well browned. Put into a casserole with the pan juices. Peel the onions and garlic. Put into the processor bowl with the parsley and chop finely (metal blade). Sprinkle over the meat. Stir together the cider, stock and Worcestershire sauce, and season well with salt and pepper. Pour over the meat. Cover and cook at 170 °C/325 °F/Gas Mark 3 for 1½ hours. Serve with baked potatoes in their jackets and chosen vegetables.

# Liver Crumb Casserole

Cut the liver into thin slices and toss in the flour. Brown lightly in the butter. Peel the onions and chop them coarsely (metal blade). Cook in butter until soft and golden. Grease a casserole and arrange liver and onions in layers in it, sprinkling each onion layer with salt and pepper. Discard the crusts from the bread and make bread into crumbs (metal blade). Chop the parsley finely (metal blade) and mix with the crumbs. Sprinkle this mixture on top of the onions and pour on the stock. Cover and cook at 180 °C/350 °F/Gas Mark 4 for 45 minutes. Remove the lid and continue cooking for 15 minutes to brown the crumbs. Serve with a green salad or vegetables.

450 g (1 lb) lamb's or pig's liver
25 g (1 oz) plain flour
50 g (2 oz) butter
2 onions
salt and pepper
225 g (8 oz) day-old white bread
2 large sprigs of parsley
300 ml ($\frac{1}{2}$ pint) stock .

# Kidney Pudding

Skin the kidneys and remove cores. Chop them finely (metal blade). Discard the crusts from the bread. Put the bread and parsley in processor bowl and make into crumbs (metal blade). Mix the bread with the kidneys, suet, egg, milk, herbs, salt and pepper. Grease a pudding basin and put kidney mixture in it. Cover with greased greaseproof paper and foil and put into a pan. Pour in boiling water to come half-way up the bowl. Cover the pan and boil for $1\frac{1}{2}$ hours, adding more boiling water if needed so that the pan does not boil dry. Turn out and serve with gravy.

3 lambs' kidneys
100 g (4 oz) day-old white bread
1 sprig of parsley
1 tablespoon shredded suet
1 egg
5 tablespoons milk
$\frac{1}{2}$ teaspoon dried mixed herbs
salt and pepper

# Pork Olives

4 thin slices of lean pork
1 large onion
4 sage leaves
25 g (1 oz) butter
100 g (4 oz) day-old white
  bread
1 lemon
1 egg
salt and pepper
15 g (½ oz) plain flour
300 ml (½ pint) stock

Beat the pieces of pork very flat with a rolling pin. Peel the onion and with the sage leaves chop finely (metal blade). Melt the butter in a pan and cook the onion and sage for 5 minutes over low heat stirring well. Lift out of the fat and put into a mixing bowl. Discard the crusts from the bread and make bread into crumbs (metal blade). Add to the onion. Cut the lemon in half and cut one half into quarters for garnishing. Grate the rind from the other half and squeeze out the juice (juice extractor). Add the rind and juice to the breadcrumbs with the egg, salt and pepper. Mix well and divide the stuffing between the pieces of pork. Roll up and tie lightly with cotton. Dust the pork rolls with the flour and brown on all sides in the fat left in the pan. Add the stock, cover and simmer for 1½ hours. Remove cotton from the meat. Put into a serving dish, pour on the pan juices and garnish with lemon wedges.

# Country Pork

2 kg (4 lb) loin of pork
1 onion
1 eating apple
6 sage leaves
75 g (3 oz) day-old white bread
1 egg
1 tablespoon lemon juice
salt and pepper
a little oil

Have the joint boned, and ask the butcher to score the skin finely. Make a slit in the meat where the bone has been removed so that the stuffing can be inserted. Peel the onion, and peel and core the apple. Mix them with the sage leaves and chop finely (metal blade). Discard the crusts from the bread and make bread into crumbs (metal blade). Add to the onion mixture and add the egg, lemon juice, salt and pepper. Mix well and insert into the meat. Tie the joint in 3 or 4 places with string. Put into a roasting tin and rub a little oil over the skin. Sprinkle with salt and rub in. Roast at 180°C/ 350°F/Gas Mark 4 for 2½ hours.

# Pork and Apple Pudding

Mix the flour, suet, salt and water to a firm dough (plastic blade). Cut the pork into pieces and chop coarsely (metal blade). Peel and core the apples and chop coarsely with the sage (metal blade). Mix the pork and apples together and season with salt and pepper. Grease a pudding basin and use two-thirds of the dough to line it. Put in the meat mixture. Pour in the stock or water and cover with the remaining dough. Grease a piece of greaseproof paper and cover the dough. Cover again with foil. Put into a pan and pour in boiling water to come half-way up the bowl. Cover the pan and boil for 4 hours, adding more boiling water if needed so that the pan does not boil dry. Turn out and serve with gravy.

225 g (8 oz) self-raising flour
100 g (4 oz) shredded suet
pinch of salt
5 tablespoons cold water
450 g (1 lb) lean pork
2 cooking apples
3 sage leaves
salt and pepper
150 ml ($\frac{1}{4}$ pint) stock or water

# Bacon and Onion Roll

Mix the flour, suet, salt and water to a firm dough (plastic blade). Roll out on a floured board into a rectangle. Derind the bacon and peel the onion. Chop bacon, onion and sage leaves finely together (metal blade). Season with salt and pepper and spread on the dough. Roll up like a Swiss roll. Grease a piece of greaseproof paper and wrap the dough in it and then in foil. Put into a pan and pour in boiling water to cover the parcel. Cover the pan and boil for 2 hours adding more boiling water if needed so that the pan does not boil dry. Unwrap on to a serving dish and serve in thick slices with gravy.

225 g (8 oz) self-raising flour
75 g (3 oz) shredded suet
pinch of salt
4–5 tablespoons cold water
175 g (6 oz) streaky bacon
1 onion
4 sage leaves
salt and pepper

# Crépinettes

450 g (1 lb) pig's liver
350 g (12 oz) pickled belly of
  pork
1 garlic clove
1 teaspoon salt
1 teaspoon pepper
pinch of ground allspice
caul fat (optional)

When buying the liver and pork, ask the butcher for a piece of caul fat. This is a lace-like skin (called 'leaf', 'flead' or 'veiling' in some areas) from near the kidneys, and is used to cover pâtés to give them an attractive appearance and delicious flavour. It is also used to cover the popular country faggots, of which this is a special French version. The little meatballs taste like a very good pâté and may be eaten hot or cold.

Cut the liver and pork into pieces. Peel and chop the garlic. Chop finely with the liver, pork and seasonings (metal blade). Flour your hands lightly and form the mixture into 12 balls. If possible, wrap each in a small piece of caul fat. Arrange the meatballs in an ovenware dish or tin so that they just touch and the dish is full. Bake at 180°C/350°F/Gas Mark 4 for 45 minutes. Serve hot with pan juices, or leave until cold. They are very good with an accompaniment of crusty bread.

# Home-made Sausages

225 g (8 oz) lean pork
225 g (8 oz) fat belly of pork
1 garlic clove
4 sage leaves
pinch of dried thyme
½ teaspoon salt
1 teaspoon pepper

Cut the lean and fat pork into pieces. Peel and chop the garlic. Chop the pork, garlic and sage leaves, coarsely or finely according to taste (metal blade). Add thyme, salt and pepper, and process just long enough to mix. Form into sausage shapes or flat patties. Chill in the refrigerator for 12 hours before using so that the flavours blend and mature.

# Pineapple Glazed Chicken

Remove the giblets from the chicken. Keep the liver for pâté or an omelette. Cook the remaining giblets in water to make stock. Peel the onion and chop finely (metal blade). Heat half the butter and cook the onion over low heat for 5 minutes until soft and golden. Discard the crusts from the bread and make bread into crumbs (metal blade). Put into a bowl with the onion. Chop the walnuts finely (metal blade) and put into the bowl. Chop the pineapple coarsely (metal blade) and add to the bowl. Stir in the raisins, lemon rind, salt and pepper. Moisten with 2 tablespoons pineapple syrup and stuff the bird. Put into a roasting tin and spread with the remaining butter. Roast at 180°C/350°F/Gas Mark 4 for 1 hour. Pour on the remaining syrup and continue cooking for 15 minutes. Baste the chicken with the pan juices and continue cooking for 15 minutes. Lift chicken on to a serving dish. Add 150 ml ($\frac{1}{4}$ pint) giblet stock to pan juices, heat and serve separately as gravy.

1·5 kg (3 lb) chicken
1 large onion
75 g (3 oz) butter
175 g (6 oz) day-old white bread
50 g (2 oz) walnut halves
4 canned pineapple rings
50 g (2 oz) seedless raisins
$\frac{1}{2}$ teaspoon grated lemon rind
salt and pepper
6 tablespoons pineapple syrup from can

# Chestnut Chicken

Remove the giblets from the chicken and set aside the liver. Cook the remaining giblets in water to make stock for gravy. Peel the onion and chop finely with the chicken liver (metal blade). Melt half the butter in a pan and stir in the onion and liver over low heat for 5 minutes. Peel the oranges, remove white pith, and chop the flesh (metal blade). Put the onion, liver and orange flesh into a bowl. Split the hard skins of the chestnuts with a sharp knife and boil them in water for 10 minutes. Remove the hard shell and brown inner skin. Chop the chestnuts finely (metal blade) and mix with the oranges. Boil the rice in salted water for 10 minutes, drain well and add to the bowl. Mix with the egg, salt and pepper. Stuff the chicken and place in a roasting tin. Spread the remaining butter on the bird and roast at 180°C/350°F/Gas Mark 4 for $1\frac{1}{2}$ hours. Serve with gravy made from giblet stock.

1·5 kg (3 lb) chicken
1 large onion
75 g (3 oz) butter
2 oranges
225 g (8 oz) chestnuts
100 g (4 oz) long-grained rice
1 egg
salt and pepper

# Country Chicken Bake

6 chicken joints
15 g (½ oz) plain flour
25 g (1 oz) dripping
150 ml (¼ pint) dry cider
4 rashers streaky bacon
2 large onions
225 g (8 oz) day-old white
    bread
100 g (4 oz) shredded suet
pinch of dried thyme
½ teaspoon grated lemon rind
salt and pepper
1 egg
4 tablespoons milk

Dust the chicken joints in flour and brown on all sides in the dripping. Grease an ovenware dish and put chicken joints in it. Pour in the cider. Derind the bacon and chop coarsely (metal blade). Keep on one side. Peel the onions and chop finely (metal blade). Mix with the bacon. Discard the crusts from the bread and make bread into crumbs (metal blade). Add the suet, thyme, lemon rind, salt, pepper, egg and milk and mix to a soft dough (plastic blade). Add the onion and bacon and mix until just incorporated. Cover the chicken with the dough. Cover with a piece of foil and bake at 180 °C/350 °F/Gas Mark 4 for 2 hours. Remove the foil and continue cooking for 15 minutes. Serve with gravy.

# Chicken and Cheese Crumble

175 g (6 oz) cooked chicken
1 small onion
1 green pepper
25 g (1 oz) butter
25 g (1 oz) plain flour
150 ml (¼ pint) chicken stock
150 ml (¼ pint) milk
1 teaspoon Worcestershire
    sauce
salt and pepper

*Topping*
50 g (2 oz) Cheddar cheese
75 g (3 oz) plain flour
40 g (1½ oz) butter
salt and pepper
pinch of mustard powder

Chop the chicken coarsely (metal blade). Peel the onion and chop finely (metal blade). Remove the stem and seeds from the pepper and chop the flesh coarsely (metal blade). Melt the butter in a pan and stir in the onion and pepper over low heat for 5 minutes. Stir in the flour and cook for 1 minute. Take off the heat and stir in the stock and milk. Bring to the boil, stirring well, and cook for 1 minute. Add the chicken, Worcestershire sauce, salt and pepper and put into an ovenware dish. Chop the cheese coarsely (metal blade). Add the flour, butter, salt, pepper and mustard. Continue processing until the mixture is like crumbs. Sprinkle on the chicken. Bake at 190 °C/375 °F/Gas Mark 5 for 45 minutes.

# Southern Chicken

Chop the chicken coarsely (metal blade). Peel the onion and chop finely (metal blade). Wipe the mushrooms and chop coarsely (metal blade). Heat the oil in a pan and stir the onion and mushrooms over low heat for 5 minutes. Chop the parsley and olives finely (metal blade). Add to the onion mixture. Sieve the tomatoes and their juice and add to the pan with the chicken stock. Simmer for 10 minutes, stirring well. Add the chopped chicken and continue heating and stirring for 10 minutes. Serve on a bed of rice or pasta with a green salad.

450 g (1 lb) cooked chicken
1 small onion
100 g (4 oz) button mushrooms
3 tablespoons oil
2 large sprigs of parsley
8 Spanish stuffed olives
225 g (8 oz) canned tomatoes
450 ml ($\frac{3}{4}$ pint) chicken stock

# Summer Chicken Curry

Chop the chicken coarsely (metal blade) and keep on one side. Put the coconut into a bowl and pour on the boiling water. Leave to soak. Peel the onion and chop it finely (metal blade). Melt the butter in a pan and stir the onion over low heat for 5 minutes until soft and golden. Stir in the flour, curry powder and paste and cook gently for 5 minutes. Strain the liquid from the coconut and add to the mixture with the chicken stock. Stir well until creamy and then simmer for 30 minutes. Peel and core the apple and pear and chop coarsely (metal blade). Peel the banana and slice (disc H). Add the apple, pear and banana to the sauce with the chicken. Chop the apricots coarsely (metal blade), mix with the sultanas, cover with hot water and leave for 5 minutes. Drain and add to the chicken mixture. Simmer for 5 minutes. Remove from heat and stir in the cream, lemon juice and salt. Serve hot with boiled rice, popadums and chutney. This curry is also delicious if chilled and served with rice salad.

350 g (12 oz) cooked chicken
25 g (1 oz) desiccated coconut
150 ml ($\frac{1}{4}$ pint) boiling water
1 onion
50 g (2 oz) butter
25 g (1 oz) plain flour
2 teaspoons curry powder
1 teaspoon curry paste
600 ml (1 pint) chicken stock
1 eating apple
1 eating pear
1 banana
50 g (2 oz) dried apricots
50 g (2 oz) sultanas
5 tablespoons double cream
2 tablespoons lemon juice
pinch of salt

# Pizza

225 g (8 oz) once-risen bread
    dough (page 118)
a little olive oil
350 g (12 oz) Mozzarella or
    Cheddar cheese
450 g (1 lb) tomatoes
1 teaspoon chopped fresh
    marjoram, thyme or basil
pepper
75 g (3 oz) anchovy fillets
black olives

The bread dough should have risen until double in size. Turn on to a board and flatten into a long strip. Brush with a little oil and roll up like a Swiss roll. Repeat this process 3 times. Divide the dough into 4 pieces and roll each piece to a flat circle 18 cm (7 in) across. Oil 4 flan tins (or a baking sheet), and put dough in them. Brush surface of dough with olive oil. Cut the cheese in thin slices or grate (disc A) and arrange half on the surface of the dough. Skin the tomatoes by dipping them in boiling water. Slice them and put on top of the cheese then cover with remaining cheese. Sprinkle with herbs and pepper. Drain anchovy fillets and arrange in a lattice on each pizza. Garnish with olives and sprinkle with a little olive oil. Bake at 230 °C/450 °F/Gas Mark 8 for 25 minutes.

### Pizza Sorrento

Prepare pizza as above but omit anchovy fillets and olives from topping. Instead, arrange 100 g (4 oz) sliced salami and 1 chopped green pepper on top of the tomatoes and cheese. Sprinkle with a little olive oil and bake as above.

### Pizza San Remo

Prepare the dough as above. Chop 450 g (1 lb) onions coarsely and cook in 50 g (2 oz) butter for 15 minutes. Season to taste and spread on dough. Drain a can of sardines and place fish on top. Garnish with black olives and bake as above.

### Pizza Francescana

Cover dough with 100 g (4 oz) thinly sliced Bel Paese cheese, 225 g (8 oz) chopped cooked ham, 100 g (4 oz) chopped mushrooms and 225 g (8 oz) sliced tomatoes. Season well, sprinkle with oil and bake as above.

# Cheese Soufflé

Grate the Cheddar cheese (disc A) and keep on one side. Put the egg yolks into the processor bowl. Add the flour, milk, salt, pepper and mustard and mix until smooth (plastic blade). Melt the butter and pour in the mixture. Stir gently over low heat until thick and creamy. Cool slightly and put into the processor bowl with the Cheddar cheese. Mix until the cheese is incorporated (plastic blade), then turn into another bowl. Whisk the egg whites to stiff peaks (whisk attachment). Fold into the cheese mixture. Thoroughly grease a 1·2 litre (2 pint) soufflé dish and put the cheese mixture in it. Grate the Parmesan cheese (disc A) and sprinkle on top. Bake at 190 °C/375 °F/Gas Mark 5 for 45 minutes. Serve at once.

100 g (4 oz) Cheddar cheese
3 large eggs, separated
50 g (2 oz) plain flour
300 ml ($\frac{1}{2}$ pint) milk
salt and pepper
pinch of mustard powder
50 g (2 oz) butter
15 g ($\frac{1}{2}$ oz) Parmesan cheese

# Baked Cheese Pudding

Discard the crusts from the bread and make bread into crumbs (metal blade). Grate the cheese (disc A). Chop the onion finely (metal blade). Put the milk and butter into a pan and heat until the butter has just melted. Pour over the bread and leave to soak for 30 minutes. Stir in the egg yolks, cheese and onion, and season well. Whisk the egg whites to stiff peaks (whisk attachment) and fold into the crumbs. Grease an ovenware dish and bake at 180 °C/350 °F/Gas Mark 4 for 1 hour. Serve hot with vegetables, or leave until cold, turn out and serve with salad.

175 g (6 oz) day-old white
  bread
100 g (4 oz) Cheddar cheese
1 small onion
600 ml (1 pint) milk
50 g (2 oz) butter
2 eggs, separated
salt and pepper

1. Chipping potatoes
2. Chopping red pepper
3. Adding eggs to pan

# Spanish Omelette

2 potatoes
1 small red pepper
1 small onion
4 mushrooms
2 tablespoons cooking oil
50 g (2 oz) cooked peas
4 eggs
2 tablespoons water
salt and pepper
25 g (1 oz) butter
1 sprig of parsley

Peel the potatoes and chip them (disc E). Put into cold water, bring to the boil and boil for 5 minutes. Drain well. Cut the pepper in half and remove the stem and seeds. Peel the onion and wipe the mushrooms. Chop the pepper, onion and mushrooms coarsely (metal blade). Heat the oil in a heavy-based frying pan and cook the potato pieces over gentle heat until golden and soft. Add pepper, onion and mushrooms and stir together over low heat until soft but not coloured. Stir in the peas. While the vegetables are cooking, mix the eggs with the water, salt and pepper until just blended (plastic blade). Add the butter to the pan and when it has just melted, pour in the eggs. Cook gently, stirring and lifting the egg mixture from the bottom of the pan. When the eggs are set but still creamy, the omelette is ready. Chop the parsley (metal blade). Sprinkle on the omelette. Serve in slices.

# 7. Vegetables and Salads

A great variety of vegetable dishes and salads may be prepared with the cutting discs. An imaginative cook will happily combine favourite ingredients, but there are two basic rules for successful salad making. Colour is particularly important – think of a winter mixture of shredded red and white cabbage, sliced leeks and Brussels sprouts, grated carrots and chopped walnuts. This kind of salad also conforms to the second rule of providing a variety of shapes and textures, which is easy with the variety of cutting discs available.

*To slice onions*, peel and cut in halves, quarters or eighths according to size. Leave shallots whole. Wedge onions firmly in the feeder tube, pointing upright. Press with the pusher, not fingers.

*To slice mushrooms*, choose firm button mushrooms. Remove any coarse stems and cut them level with the caps. Wipe with a damp cloth, without washing. Stack the mushrooms in the feeder tube. Fill the tube almost to the top and press down with the pusher.

*To shred cabbage*, cut in pieces small enough to fit the feeder tube. Fill the tube almost to the top and press down with the pusher. Make sure that red or white cabbages are really firm and tightly packed.

*To grate or slice carrots*, put the peeled carrots upright in the feeder tube and pack firmly side by side.

*To slice cucumbers*, cut lengths just smaller than the length of the feeder tube and put in two lengths at a time.

*To slice leeks*, trim and clean. Pack upright in feeder tube.

*To slice courgettes*, top and tail. Pack upright in feeder tube.

# Potato and Onion Bake

Peel and chip the potatoes (disc E). Peel and quarter the onions and slice (disc D). Grease a gratin dish with a little of the butter. Arrange a layer of half the potatoes. Season and dot with butter. Arrange the onions on top. Season and dot with butter. Cover with remaining potatoes. Season and dot with remaining butter. Pour on the milk. Cover with foil and bake at 180 °C/350 °F/Gas Mark 4 for 1 hour. Remove foil and raise heat to 190 °C/375 °F/Gas Mark 5 and continue baking for 20 minutes until golden. Serve with meat, fish or poultry.

450 g (1 lb) potatoes
225 g (8 oz) onions
50 g (2 oz) butter
salt and pepper
450 ml ($\frac{3}{4}$ pint) creamy milk

# Glazed Carrots

Scrape the carrots and slice them (disc H). Put into a pan with the other ingredients except parsley. Bring to the boil, cover and cook for 5 minutes. Remove lid and simmer until tender and the stock is absorbed. Chop the parsley (metal blade) and sprinkle over the carrots.

450 g (1 lb) carrots
300 ml ($\frac{1}{2}$ pint) chicken stock
25 g (1 oz) butter
2 teaspoons sugar
pinch of salt
1 sprig of parsley

# Ratatouille

Skin the tomatoes by dipping them in boiling water. Cut in quarters and discard seeds. Chop coarsely (metal blade). Wipe but do not peel the aubergines and cut them into large pieces. Remove stem and seeds from the pepper and cut the flesh into large pieces. Peel the onions and cut into pieces. Chop the aubergines, pepper and onions coarsely (metal blade). Wipe but do not peel the courgettes. Slice them (disc H). Put the oil and butter into a heavy-based pan and heat together. Add all the vegetables. Peel and crush the garlic and add with salt and pepper. Stir well and cover tightly. Simmer for 1 hour until the vegetables are tender and the oil has been absorbed. Chop the parsley finely (metal blade) and sprinkle thickly on top. Serve hot or cold with crusty bread, or as an accompaniment to meat, fish or poultry.

4 large tomatoes
2 aubergines
1 large green pepper
2 onions
2 courgettes
3 tablespoons olive oil
25 g (1 oz) butter
1 garlic clove
salt and pepper
2 large sprigs of parsley

# Stuffed Tomatoes

6 large tomatoes
1 small onion
1 tablespoon oil
225 g (8 oz) canned tuna fish
50 g (2 oz) anchovy fillets
100 g (4 oz) day-old white
  bread
2 large sprigs of parsley
4 Spanish stuffed olives
salt and pepper

Remove lids from the tomatoes by cutting them across one-third of the way down. Scoop out the pulp and discard seeds. Peel the onion and chop finely (metal blade). Heat the oil in a pan and cook onions until soft and golden. Drain the tuna fish and anchovy fillets. Chop coarsely (metal blade). Put into a bowl with the cooked onion. Discard the crusts from the bread and make bread into crumbs (metal blade). Add to the fish. Chop the parsley and olives finely (metal blade). Add to the fish and stir in the tomato pulp and juice. Season well. Fill the tomato bases and replace the lids lightly. Grease an ovenware dish and put the tomatoes in it. Bake at 190 °C/375 °F/Gas Mark 5 for 15 minutes. Serve hot or cold.

# Lentil Purée

450 g (1 lb) lentils
1 potato
1 onion
1 carrot
600 ml (1 pint) bacon stock
1 bay leaf
1 sprig of thyme or marjoram
50 g (2 oz) butter
6 tablespoons single cream
pepper

Put the lentils into a bowl and cover with cold water. Leave to soak overnight. Drain the lentils and put into the processor bowl. Chop finely (metal blade). Put into a saucepan. Peel the potato, onion and carrot, and chop coarsely (metal blade). Add to the pan with the bacon stock, bay leaf, thyme or marjoram. Bring to the boil, then cover and simmer for 1 hour, when the liquid should be almost absorbed. Drain well and remove the herbs. Cool slightly and blend until smooth (blender attachment). Add the butter and cream and blend again until completely mixed. Return to a clean saucepan and heat through. Season to taste with pepper. By processing lentils and vegetables first, cooking time is shortened considerably. The potato will remove excess saltiness from the bacon stock.

# Swiss Potato Cake

1 kg (2 lb) potatoes
1 onion
75 g (3 oz) butter
50 g (2 oz) Gruyère cheese
salt and pepper

Wash the potatoes and boil them in their skins for 10 minutes. Cool and peel. Cut into large pieces and grate (disc C). Peel the onion and chop finely (metal blade). Melt half the butter in a pan and cook the onion for 5 minutes until soft. Add the remaining butter and then the potatoes. Grate the cheese (disc A) and add to the mixture. Season and stir well. Press the mixture down firmly with a palette knife and cook for about 10 minutes until golden brown underneath. Turn the potato cake over carefully with a fish slice and continue cooking for 10 minutes. Serve cut into wedges.

# Sweet and Sour Red Cabbage

Remove outer leaves from the cabbage and take out the hard stem. Wash and shred the cabbage (disc H). Peel the onions and chop finely (metal blade). Peel and core the apple and chop coarsely (metal blade). Melt the butter in a pan and cook the onion for 5 minutes over low heat, stirring well. Add the sugar and vinegar and put in the cabbage. Stir well and add the cider, salt and pepper. Cover and simmer for 1 hour. Stir in the apple pieces and continue cooking for 1 hour. If preferred, the cabbage may be cooked in the oven at 170 °C/325 °F/Gas Mark 3 for 2 hours. It is particularly good with sausages, pork or duck.

1 kg (2 lb) red cabbage
2 small onions
1 eating apple
15 g (½ oz) butter
1 tablespoon dark soft brown sugar
1 tablespoon vinegar
300 ml (½ pint) dry cider
salt and pepper

# Courgettes in Tomato Sauce

Wipe but do not peel the courgettes. Slice them (disc H) and keep on one side. Peel the onion and garlic clove and chop finely (metal blade). Heat the oil in a pan and cook the onion and garlic over low heat, stirring well, for 5 minutes, until golden and soft. Stir in the tomatoes and their juice, tomato purée, lemon juice, sugar, salt and pepper. Bring to the boil, then simmer and stir for 10 minutes. Stir in the sliced courgettes. Grease a 1·2 litre (2 pint) casserole and pour the mixture into it. Discard the crusts from the bread and make bread into crumbs (metal blade). Grate the cheese (disc A). Chop the parsley (metal blade). Mix the crumbs, cheese and parsley and season lightly with salt and pepper. Sprinkle over the courgette mixture. Bake at 200 °C/400 °F/Gas Mark 6 for 30 minutes. Serve as a dish on its own, or as an accompaniment to meat or fish.

1 kg (2 lb) courgettes
1 large onion
1 garlic clove
2 tablespoons oil
450 g (1 lb) canned tomatoes
1 tablespoon tomato purée
1 teaspoon lemon juice
1 teaspoon sugar
salt and pepper
50 g (2 oz) day-old white bread
25 g (1 oz) Cheddar cheese
1 large sprig of parsley

# Greek Mushrooms

450 g (1 lb) button mushrooms
100 g (4 oz) onions
4 tablespoons olive oil
150 ml (¼ pint) white wine
1 lemon
1 sprig of parsley
1 sprig of thyme
1 bay leaf
pinch of salt
few grains of coriander
4 white peppercorns

Wipe the mushrooms and slice (disc H). Peel the onions and chop finely (metal blade). Heat the oil and cook the onions over low heat for 5 minutes, stirring well. Add the mushrooms and wine. Squeeze the juice from the lemon (juice extractor) and add to the pan. Add the herbs, salt, coriander and peppercorns and bring to the boil. Cover and simmer for 6 minutes. Take off the lid and continue simmering for 4 minutes. Remove the herbs and peppercorns, put into a serving dish and chill for 2 hours. Serve with crusty bread.

# Waldorf Salad

4 red-skinned eating apples
2 teaspoons lemon juice
½ cucumber
3 celery sticks
75 g (3 oz) walnut halves
2 sprigs of parsley
150 ml (¼ pint) mayonnaise
crisp lettuce leaves
watercress sprigs

Wipe and core the apples but do not peel them. Cut into quarters and chop coarsely (metal blade). Put into a bowl and sprinkle with lemon juice. Peel the cucumber and chop coarsely (metal blade). Wash and trim the celery and chop coarsely with the walnuts (metal blade). Mix the cucumber, celery and walnuts with the apples. Chop the parsley (metal blade) and add to the mixture. Stir in the mayonnaise until the pieces are well-coated. Arrange the lettuce leaves on a serving dish and pile the salad in the centre. Garnish with watercress sprigs.

# Jellied Beetroot Salad

4 beetroot
1 small onion
1 raspberry jelly tablet
300 ml (½ pint) white vinegar
300 ml (½ pint) water

Cook the beetroot, cool and rub off the skins. Chop coarsely (metal blade). Peel the onion and chop finely (metal blade). Mix the beetroot and onion together in a bowl. Melt the jelly tablet in boiling vinegar and water and pour over the beetroot. Leave until set and then break up lightly with a fork.

# Fresh Spinach Salad with Bacon Dressing

Wash the spinach thoroughly and remove the stalks. Pat the leaves dry with kitchen paper. Chop coarsely (metal blade) and put into a salad bowl. Derind the bacon and chop coarsely (metal blade). Put into a heavy-based pan and heat until the fat runs. Let the bacon cook until crisp, then lift it from the fat with a slotted spoon and add to the spinach. Discard the crusts from the bread and break bread into pieces. Process (metal blade) until just broken into small pieces but not crumbs. Peel and crush the garlic. Toss the bread and garlic in the bacon fat until the pieces of bread are crisp and golden. Put the oil, lemon juice, mustard, salt and pepper into the processor bowl and mix thoroughly (plastic blade). Drain the bread pieces and garlic and add to the salad bowl. Pour on the dressing, toss quickly and serve at once.

1 kg (2 lb) spinach
8 rashers streaky bacon
100 g (4 oz) day-old white
   bread
1 garlic clove
6 tablespoons oil
3 tablespoons lemon juice
$\frac{1}{4}$ teaspoon French mustard
salt and pepper

# Hot Cabbage Salad

Use a cabbage which is very crisp and firm. Remove outer leaves and hard stems and cut into wedges. Wash and shred the cabbage (disc H) and put into a bowl of ice-chilled water for 30 minutes. Drain well and pat dry with kitchen paper. Mix the egg yolks lightly (plastic blade). With the machine running, add the other ingredients through the feeder tube until well blended. Put the mixture into a bowl over hot water or the top of a double saucepan. Stir constantly until creamy. Put the cabbage into a pan and pour over the sauce. Heat through and serve hot with cold meat.

1 small white cabbage
2 egg yolks
15 g ($\frac{1}{2}$ oz) softened butter
2 tablespoons cold water
2 tablespoons hot vinegar
salt and pepper

# Cucumber Salad

Peel the cucumber and slice (disc D). Sprinkle the cucumber slices with salt and leave for 30 minutes. Rinse and drain thoroughly. Mix the sugar with the vinegar and water and a shake of pepper. Pour over the cucumber and leave to stand in the refrigerator for 1 hour. Drain off the liquid and toss the cucumber in yogurt. Chop the parsley finely (metal blade) and sprinkle on the top. Serve chilled.

1 cucumber
salt and pepper
1 teaspoon sugar
150 ml ($\frac{1}{4}$ pint) white vinegar
150 ml ($\frac{1}{4}$ pint) water
150 ml ($\frac{1}{4}$ pint) natural yogurt
2 large sprigs of parsley

1. Slicing cabbage

2. Grating carrots

3. Chopping walnuts

# Cabbage and Carrot Coleslaw

450 g (1 lb) firm white cabbage
2 celery sticks
½ small onion
2 carrots
1 eating apple
50 g (2 oz) walnut halves
4 tablespoons mayonnaise
2 tablespoons single cream
1 tablespoon vinegar
pinch of mustard powder

Wash and trim the cabbage and celery. Peel the onion, carrots and apple, and remove the apple core. Shred the cabbage, slice the onion and celery (disc D). Grate the carrots (disc A). Grate the apple (disc C). Put all the prepared vegetables into a bowl. Chop the walnuts (metal blade). Add the apple and nuts to the vegetables. Stir together the mayonnaise, cream, vinegar and mustard. Pour over the other ingredients and toss well so that the dressing is mixed right through the salad.

# Avocado Salad

2 oranges
2 large sprigs of parsley
3 tablespoons oil
1 tablespoon white wine
   vinegar
salt and pepper
2 avocados

Grate the rind from one orange, and squeeze out the juice (juice extractor). Peel the other orange and divide into segments, removing all pith and skin. Mix the orange juice and rind, parsley, oil, vinegar, salt and pepper to a smooth dressing (plastic blade). Cut the avocados in half lengthways, take out the stones, and scoop out the flesh. Cut the flesh into small pieces and mix with the orange segments. Fill the avocado skins and pour over the dressing. Serve at once.

# Health Salad

2 red-skinned eating apples
2 celery sticks
1 carrot
½ lemon
50 g (2 oz) peanuts
50 g (2 oz) seedless raisins
4 tablespoons mayonnaise
watercress sprigs

Wipe but do not peel the apples. Cut them in quarters and remove the cores. Chop coarsely (metal blade). Wash, trim and slice the celery thinly (disc D). Peel the carrot and grate (disc A). Mix the apples, celery and carrot. Squeeze out the lemon juice (juice extractor) and sprinkle over the salad so that the apples do not discolour. Chop the peanuts coarsely (metal blade). Add to the salad with the raisins. Toss in the mayonnaise and garnish with watercress sprigs.

# Winter Salad

½ small red cabbage
2 carrots
1 leek
2 celery sticks
50 g (2 oz) walnut halves
6 tablespoons mayonnaise
2 tablespoons lemon juice
salt and pepper

Remove outer leaves from cabbage and cut out the hard stem. Wash and slice the cabbage (disc H). Peel the carrots and grate (disc A). Clean the leek thoroughly and wash and trim the celery. Slice thinly (disc D). Chop the walnuts coarsely (metal blade). Mix all the vegetables and nuts in a bowl. Mix the mayonnaise, lemon juice, salt and pepper and combine with the salad ingredients. Mix thoroughly.

# 8. Pastry, Pies and Flans

Many people find pastry-making difficult, because the dough can be affected by warm hands, over-mixing, or the addition of too much water. With a food processor, however, the making of pastry can be carefully controlled so that the correct consistency is obtained, and the speed of the operation ensures that the pastry will remain cool. Shortcrust and quick flaky pastry may be easily prepared, and so can the more tricky hot water crust pastry for raised pies. With slight adjustments to ingredients, savoury and sweet flan pastries are also made more easily and less messily than by hand.

The plastic blade is normally used for making pastry, but if the fat is particularly hard and cold the metal blade should be used. Block margarine is excellent or a mixture of lard and block margarine. For sweet flan pastry, butter gives an especially delicious flavour. Soft margarine is unsuitable for pastry making. To make pastry successfully in the food processor, do not use more than 225 g (8 oz) flour. Put flour, salt and any sugar into the bowl. Add the fat cut into 2·5 cm (1 in) pieces and process until the fat has been cut into the flour and the mixture looks like breadcrumbs. Add cold liquid through the feeder tube with the machine running, until the mixture forms a ball round the mixing blade. This pastry requires slightly less liquid than hand-made pastry and it is a good idea to keep back a little of the liquid recommended in the recipe as the pastry ball may form before it has all been added. This pastry is very light and easy to handle and roll out.

# Shortcrust Pastry

225 g (8 oz) plain flour
pinch of salt
50 g (2 oz) lard
50 g (2 oz) block margarine
3 tablespoons cold water

Put the flour and salt into the processor bowl. Cut the lard and margarine into cubes and add to the flour. Process until mixture is like fine breadcrumbs (plastic blade). With machine switched on, add water through the feeder tube to make a firm dough. Roll out and use as required.

### Wholemeal Pastry

Substitute plain wholemeal flour for white flour. It may be necessary to scrape down the bowl once or twice during processing as wholemeal flour tends to fly about the bowl. Add a little more water if necessary as wholemeal flour is a little more absorbent than white.

### Savoury Pastry

Add 50 g (2 oz) grated Cheddar cheese to the flour. Season with a pinch of pepper and a pinch of mustard powder.

# Quick Flaky Pastry

225 g (8 oz) plain flour
pinch of salt
150 g (5 oz) block margarine,
   well chilled
100 ml (4 fl oz) cold water,
   well chilled

Put the flour and salt into the processor bowl. Cut the margarine into 4 pieces and put 1 piece into the bowl. Process until the mixture is like fine breadcrumbs (plastic blade). With the machine running, add the water gradually through the feeder tube until a ball of dough forms. With a knife, divide the ball of dough into 4 pieces while still in the bowl. Cut the remaining margarine into tiny pieces and sprinkle between the sections of dough. Process just long enough to mix in the margarine. Put on to a well floured board and roll 5 mm (¼ in) thick. Fold over the top and bottom of the dough and half-turn to the right. Roll out and fold again, and half-turn to the right. Roll out and fold again, half-turn to the right. Roll out once more and fold. Cover and chill for 30 minutes, then roll out and use.

# Hot Water Crust Pastry

Put the flour and salt into the processor bowl. Heat the lard and liquid together in a pan until the fat melts. Bring to the boil. With the machine running, pour the hot liquid through the feeder tube and process to make a soft dough (plastic blade). Turn on to a lightly floured surface and knead until smooth and free from cracks. Use while warm to make savoury raised pies. This pastry becomes stiff and difficult to handle as it cools. To keep it warm, wrap in polythene and keep in a warm place.

350 g (12 oz) plain flour
1 teaspoon salt
100 g (4 oz) lard
150 ml (¼ pint) milk and water mixed

# Sweet Shortcrust Pastry

Put the flour, semolina, salt and sugar into the processor bowl. Cut the butter into pieces and add to the flour. Process until the mixture is like coarse breadcrumbs (plastic blade). Mix the egg yolk and water together. With the machine running, add the liquid through the feeder tube and process just long enough for the dough to form. Chill for 30 minutes before rolling out. Roll carefully as this pastry is rather fragile. It is particularly good for fruit tarts, and the addition of a little semolina gives a perfect texture to the pastry.

200 g (7 oz) plain flour
25 g (1 oz) fine semolina
pinch of salt
25 g (1 oz) caster sugar
100 g (4 oz) butter
1 egg yolk
3 tablespoons cold water

# Suet Pastry

Put the flour, salt and suet into the processor bowl. With the machine running, pour the water through the feeder tube until the dough forms (plastic blade). The pastry should be soft but not sticky, so add the water slowly – you may not need it all. Knead lightly on a floured board and roll out or form into dumplings. This pastry may be boiled, steamed or baked.

225 g (8 oz) self-raising flour
1 teaspoon salt
100 g (4 oz) shredded suet
150 ml (¼ pint) cold water

# Pork Pie

675 g (1½ lb) made hot water
  crust pastry (page 87)
1 kg (2 lb) shoulder pork
100 g (4 oz) unsmoked bacon
1 teaspoon chopped fresh sage
salt and pepper
pinch of ground nutmeg
3 drops anchovy essence
300 ml (½ pint) jellied stock
beaten egg for glazing

Line an 18 cm (7 in) cake tin with three-quarters of the pastry. Cut the meat in pieces and then chop finely (metal blade). Keep on one side. Chop the bacon and sage together finely (metal blade) and mix with the pork. Season well with salt and pepper, nutmeg and anchovy essence. Fill the pastry case with this mixture and moisten with 3 tablespoons stock. Cover with a lid of the remaining pastry and decorate with trimmings. Make a small hole in the centre of the lid. Brush with beaten egg. Bake at 220 °C/425 °F/Gas Mark 7 for 30 minutes. Reduce heat to 170 °C/325 °F/Gas Mark 3 for 1½ hours. Cover with greaseproof paper or foil if the pastry gets too brown. Leave in the tin to cool. After 45 minutes, pour cool liquid stock into the hole in the lid. Leave until completely cold before removing from the tin.

# Veal and Ham Pie

450 g (1 lb) made hot water
  crust pastry (page 87)
450 g (1 lb) pie veal
100 g (4 oz) raw ham or lean
  bacon
pinch of dried thyme
salt and pepper
1 hard-boiled egg, shelled
300 ml (½ pint) jellied stock
beaten egg for glazing

Prepare the pastry and use three-quarters of it to line a 450 g (1 lb) loaf tin. (If possible, use a tin with sides that unclip, which makes removal much easier.) Cut the veal and ham or bacon into pieces and chop coarsely (metal blade). Mix with the thyme, salt and pepper. Put half the meat mixture into the pastry case and place the egg in the centre. Cover with the remaining meat. Add 2 tablespoons stock. Cover with a lid of the remaining pastry and decorate with any trimmings. Make a small hole in the centre of the lid. Brush with beaten egg. Bake at 220 °C/425 °F/Gas Mark 7 for 30 minutes. Reduce heat to 170 °C/325 °F/Gas Mark 3 and continue cooking for 1½ hours. Cover the pastry with greaseproof paper or foil if it browns too quickly. Remove from the oven and leave in the tin. After 45 minutes, put a small funnel into the hole in the lid. Heat the stock until it is just liquid. Spoon into the pie through the funnel. Leave until completely cold before removing from the tin.

# Chicken and Mushroom Pie

Make up the shortcrust pastry and white sauce. Chop chicken coarsely (metal blade). Wipe and slice the mushrooms (disc H). Melt the butter in a pan and soften the mushrooms for 4 minutes. Stir the chicken and mushrooms into the sauce. Chop the parsley finely (metal blade). Add the herbs to mixture and season to taste. Put into a 1·2 litre (2 pint) pie-dish. Cover with the pastry and decorate edges. Brush well with beaten egg. Bake at 230°C/450°F/Gas Mark 8 for 15 minutes, then reduce the temperature to 190°C/375°F/Gas Mark 5 and bake for 20 minutes.

350 g (12 oz) made shortcrust pastry (page 86)
600 ml (1 pint) white sauce made with chicken stock (page 141)
350 g (12 oz) cooked chicken
175 g (6 oz) button mushrooms
25 g (1 oz) butter
1 sprig of parsley
pinch of dried thyme
salt and pepper
beaten egg for glazing

# Beef and Bacon Plate Pie

Divide the pastry into 2 pieces and roll into 2 circles to fit a 20 cm (8 in) pie-plate. Line the pie-plate with 1 piece of pastry. Chop the onion finely (metal blade) and set aside. Cut the bacon into pieces and chop finely (metal blade). Put the bacon and onion into a pan and cook gently until the fat runs from the bacon and the onion is soft and golden. Cut the steak into pieces and chop finely (metal blade). Add to the bacon and onion and stir over low heat for 5 minutes until brown. Stir in the flour and cook for 1 minute. Add the water, salt, pepper and herbs; mix well and simmer for 10 minutes. Leave until cold, and then put into the pastry case. Cover with the remaining pastry and brush with egg. Bake at 200°C/400°F/Gas Mark 6 for 30 minutes. Serve hot or cold.

350 g (12 oz) made shortcrust pastry (page 86)
1 onion
225 g (8 oz) bacon
225 g (8 oz) chuck steak
15 g ($\frac{1}{2}$ oz) plain flour
150 ml ($\frac{1}{4}$ pint) water
salt and pepper
pinch of dried mixed herbs
beaten egg for glazing

# Devonshire Onion Cream Pie

Divide the pastry into 2 pieces and roll out 2 circles to fit a 20 cm (8 in) pie-plate. Line the plate with 1 piece of pastry. Peel the onions. Chop onions and parsley together finely (metal blade). Fill the pastry case with this mixture. Cover with the cream. Put on the pastry lid and seal the edges well. Brush the lid with beaten egg. Bake at 180°C/350°F/Gas Mark 4 for 1 hour. Serve hot on its own, or with vegetables or cold meat or poultry.

350 g (12 oz) made shortcrust pastry (page 86)
2 large onions
2 large sprigs of parsley
150 ml ($\frac{1}{4}$ pint) double cream
beaten egg for glazing

1. Combining flour, fats and water into a pastry dough

2. Adding sliced apples to half the chopped pork

3. Decorating pie with pastry leaves made from trimmings

# Cheshire Pork Pie

225 g (8 oz) plain flour
pinch of salt
50 g (2 oz) block margarine
50 g (2 oz) lard
3–4 tablespoons cold water
1 kg (2 lb) lean pork
4 eating apples
salt and pepper
pinch of ground nutmeg
25 g (1 oz) sugar
150 ml ($\frac{1}{4}$ pint) dry white wine
 or dry cider
75 g (3 oz) butter
beaten egg for glazing

Put the flour and salt into the mixer bowl (plastic blade). Cut the fats into cubes and add to the flour. Mix for 10 seconds until the mixture is like fine breadcrumbs. With machine switched on, add just enough water through feeder tube to make a firm dough. Roll the pastry into 2 circles to fit a 25 cm (10 in) pie-plate.

Cut the meat into pieces and chop (metal blade). Peel and core the apples and slice (disc H). Line the plate with 1 piece of pastry. Put in half the pork and season with salt, pepper and nutmeg. Put the apples on top and sprinkle with sugar. Top with remaining pork and season with salt, pepper and nutmeg. Pour on the wine or cider and dot the pork with flakes of butter. Cover with the remaining pastry and cut a slit on top. Surround with pastry leaves made from trimmings. Add a pinch of salt to the beaten egg and brush the pastry. Bake at 220 °C/425 °F/Gas Mark 7 for 15 minutes. Reduce heat to 190 °C/375 °F/Gas Mark 5 for a further 45 minutes. Serve hot.

# Curry Pies

350 g (12 oz) made quick flaky
    pastry (page 86)
1 small onion
225 g (8 oz) cooked lamb
1 small eating apple
15 g ($\frac{1}{2}$ oz) lard
15 g ($\frac{1}{2}$ oz) plain flour
1 teaspoon curry powder
300 ml ($\frac{1}{2}$ pint) stock
25 g (1 oz) desiccated coconut
25 g (1 oz) sultanas
salt and pepper
beaten egg for glazing

Roll out the pastry and cut out 16 rounds to line and provide lids for 8 large tartlet tins. Line the tins. Peel and chop the onion finely (metal blade) and keep on one side. Cut the lamb into pieces and chop finely (metal blade) and keep on one side. Peel and core the apple and chop finely (metal blade). Melt the lard in a pan and cook the onion over low heat for 5 minutes until golden. Stir in the flour and curry powder and cook for 1 minute, stirring well. Add the stock and stir over low heat until the mixture comes to the boil and thickens. Add the meat, apple, coconut and sultanas and season well. Heat through for 10 minutes and then cool. Divide the mixture between the pastry cases. Put on pastry lids and seal edges well. Make a small hole in the lids with a skewer. Brush with a little beaten egg and bake at 200 °C/400 °F/Gas Mark 6 for 30 minutes.

# Spiced Beef Puffs

350 g (12 oz) made quick flaky
    pastry (page 86)
1 onion
225 g (8 oz) chuck steak
1 small green pepper
6 Spanish stuffed olives
1 tablespoon oil
15 g ($\frac{1}{2}$ oz) butter
1 tablespoon tomato purée
pinch of ground ginger
pinch of chilli powder
salt and pepper
beaten egg for glazing

Roll out the pastry and cut out eight 15 cm (6 in) rounds. Peel and chop the onion finely (metal blade) and keep on one side. Chop the chuck steak finely (metal blade) and keep on one side. Remove stem and seeds from the pepper and chop flesh finely with the olives. Heat the oil and butter together in a pan and cook the onion over low heat for 5 minutes until soft and golden. Stir in the meat and continue cooking for 5 minutes, stirring all the time. Add the pepper and olives, tomato purée, ginger, chilli powder, salt and pepper. Cover and cook on low heat for 10 minutes. Drain off surplus fat and leave the meat mixture to cool. Divide the mixture between the pastry circles and dampen the edges of the pastry. Fold over and seal edges firmly. Chill for 30 minutes. Brush tops with beaten egg and bake at 220 °C/425 °F/Gas Mark 7 for 20 minutes. Serve hot or cold.

# Pork Pasties

Roll out the pastry and cut into eight 15 cm (6 in) rounds. Cut the pork into pieces and chop finely (metal blade). Keep on one side. Peel and core the apples and chop the flesh finely (metal blade). Mix with the pork. Chop the eggs finely and mix with meat. Peel and chop the onion finely with the sage and add to the meat. Season well. Divide the mixture between the pastry circles and wet the edges of the pastry. Fold over and seal the edges well. Grease a baking sheet and put the pasties on it. Brush each pasty with beaten egg. Bake at 220 °C/425 °F/Gas Mark 7 for 30 minutes. Serve hot or cold.

350 g (12 oz) made shortcrust pastry (page 86)
225 g (8 oz) cooked pork
2 eating apples
2 hard-boiled eggs, shelled
1 small onion
3 sage leaves
salt and pepper
beaten egg for glazing

# Cheese and Apple Roll

Roll out the pastry to a 30 cm (12 in) square. Peel and chop the onion finely (metal blade). Melt the butter in a pan and cook the onion for 5 minutes until soft and golden. Peel and core the apple and chop finely (metal blade). Grate the cheese (disc A). Sprinkle the cheese on the pastry, leaving a 1 cm (½ in) edge. Sprinkle the onion and apple on the cheese and season with salt and pepper. Brush the pastry edges with beaten egg. Roll up the pastry loosely like a Swiss roll. Grease a baking sheet and put the pastry on it with the join underneath. Tuck in the edges. Brush with beaten egg. Make 6 slits across the top with a sharp knife. Bake at 220 °C/425 °F/Gas Mark 7 for 35 minutes. Serve hot.

350 g (12 oz) made quick flaky pastry (page 86)
1 large onion
15 g (½ oz) butter
1 large eating apple
225 g (8 oz) Gouda cheese
salt and pepper
beaten egg for glazing

# Blue Cheese Flan

225 g (8 oz) made shortcrust
   pastry (page 86)
100 g (4 oz) Danish blue cheese
225 g (8 oz) onions
75 g (3 oz) butter
40 g (1½ oz) plain flour
300 ml (½ pint) milk
salt and pepper
pinch of mustard powder

Roll out the pastry to line a 20 cm (8 in) flan tin. Roll out trimmings and cut into 1 cm (½ in) strips to use for a lattice. Chop the cheese (metal blade) and keep on one side. Peel and chop the onions finely (metal blade). Melt half the butter in a pan and cook the onions over low heat for 5 minutes until soft and golden. Lift the onions from the pan with a slotted spoon and keep on one side. Add the remaining butter to the pan, melt and stir in the flour. Cook for 1 minute and add the milk gradually. Stir over low heat until creamy. Add salt, pepper and mustard and stir in the onions. Take off the heat and stir in the cheese. Leave until cool. Put into the pastry case and arrange a pastry lattice on top. Bake at 220 °C/425 °F/Gas Mark 7 for 15 minutes. Reduce heat to 180 °C/350 °F/Gas Mark 4 for 25 minutes. Serve hot.

# Cheese and Vegetable Flan

225 g (8 oz) made shortcrust
   pastry (page 86)
100 g (4 oz) carrots
100 g (4 oz) French beans
1 small onion
1 small green pepper
100 g (4 oz) back bacon
100 g (4 oz) tomatoes
50 g (2 oz) butter
salt and pepper
175 g (6 oz) Gouda cheese

Roll out the pastry and line a 20 cm (8 in) flan tin. Scrape the carrots; top and tail the beans. Slice both (disc H). Keep on one side. Peel the onion. Remove stem and seeds from green pepper. Chop onion, green pepper and bacon finely (metal blade). Skin the tomatoes by dipping into boiling water. Cut into quarters and discard the seeds. Chop the flesh coarsely (metal blade). Melt the butter in a pan and cook the bacon and vegetables for 10 minutes over low heat, stirring well. Season with salt and pepper and leave until cold. Put into the pastry case and cover the vegetables with a piece of foil. Bake at 200 °C/400 °F/Gas Mark 6 for 45 minutes. Grate the cheese (disc A). Remove the foil and sprinkle the cheese all over the vegetables. Continue baking for 15 minutes until the cheese has melted. Serve at once.

# 9. Puddings and Ices

Though many people welcome a sweet finish to a meal it is often difficult to think of recipes which are quick and easy to prepare. In the preparation of puddings, however, the food processor is a great boon. It can be used to make breadcrumbs or cake crumbs which lighten puddings, and will chop fruit or chocolate and whip up creamy mixtures. With the addition of the whisk attachment, egg whites may be whisked softly to fold into delicate mousses or soufflés or stiffly to make meringues. To finish the dish, cream may be whipped or a complementary sauce quickly blended.

Ice-cream making is also easy with the food processor, because the machine can be used to chop basic ingredients, whip cream and blend custard. Many recipes require ice cream to be smoothed once or twice during freezing, and the powerful action of the processor makes this a simple task.

## Apple Batter Pudding

Peel and core the apples. Chop them coarsely (metal blade). Put into a bowl with the brandy or Calvados and cinnamon and leave to stand for 1 hour. Use a little of the butter to grease an ovenware dish. Put in the apples and brandy and sprinkle with the sugar. Dot with flakes of butter. Mix the eggs, flour and milk to a thick cream (plastic blade). Pour over the fruit and bake at 200 °C/400 °F/Gas Mark 6 for 35 minutes until the batter is crisp and golden. Serve very hot with cream.

450 g (1 lb) eating apples
4 tablespoons brandy or Calvados
pinch of ground cinnamon
25 g (1 oz) butter
50 g (2 oz) light soft brown sugar
3 eggs
150 g (5 oz) self-raising flour
4 tablespoons milk

# Blackcurrant Castles

100 g (4 oz) soft margarine
100 g (4 oz) caster sugar
2 eggs
100 g (4 oz) self-raising flour
¼ teaspoon vanilla essence
2 tablespoons warm water
4 teaspoons blackcurrant jam

Mix the margarine, sugar, eggs, flour and essence to a soft consistency (plastic blade). With the motor running, add the water through the feeder tube until well mixed. Grease 4 castle pudding tins and place them on a baking sheet. Put a spoonful of jam in the base of each tin and cover with the sponge mixture. Bake at 180 °C/350 °F/Gas Mark 4 for 25 minutes. Turn out and serve hot with some additional hot blackcurrant jam.

# Apricot Pudding and Apricot Sauce

450 g (1 lb) canned apricots
175 g (6 oz) stale spongecake
150 ml (¼ pint) creamy milk
50 g (2 oz) soft margarine
50 g (2 oz) caster sugar
2 eggs, separated
finely grated rind of 1 orange
2–3 drops almond essence
3 tablespoons dark chunky marmalade

Drain the apricots and reserve the syrup. Chop 8 apricot halves coarsely (metal blade) and keep on one side. Make crumbs with the spongecake (metal blade) and put them into a bowl with the milk. Leave to stand for 10 minutes. Cream the margarine, sugar and egg yolks with the orange rind and essence (plastic blade). Add the soaked crumbs and chopped apricots and mix just long enough for them to be incorporated. Transfer to another bowl. Whisk the egg whites to soft peaks (whisk attachment) and fold into the mixture. Grease a pudding basin. Put the mixture in it. Grease a piece of greaseproof paper and cover the basin. Cover again with a piece of foil. Put into a saucepan with boiling water to come half-way up the sides of the basin. Cover the pan with a lid and boil for 2 hours, adding more boiling water from time to time so that the pan does not become dry. Turn on to a serving dish and serve with the sauce. Make this by blending the remaining apricots, juice and marmalade until smooth (blender attachment). Heat through just before serving.

# College Pudding
# and Brandy Butter

Discard the crusts from the bread and make bread into crumbs (metal blade). Keep on one side. Mix the flour, suet, spice, sugar, egg and milk to a soft dough (plastic blade). Add the crumbs and mix until just incorporated. Stir in the fruit and peel. Grease a pudding basin and put the mixture in it. Grease a piece of greaseproof paper and cover the basin. Cover again with foil. Put into a saucepan with boiling water to come half-way up the sides of the basin. Cover the pan with a lid and boil for 2 hours, adding more boiling water from time to time so that the pan does not become dry. Turn out and serve with brandy butter.

Make the brandy butter by creaming the butter with the grated lemon rind (plastic blade). With the motor running, add a little sugar and brandy alternately until completely incorporated. Put into a serving dish and chill before serving with the hot pudding.

75 g (3 oz) day-old brown
  bread
50 g (2 oz) self-raising flour
50 g (2 oz) shredded suet
$\frac{1}{2}$ teaspoon ground mixed spice
50 g (2 oz) light soft brown
  sugar
1 egg
4 tablespoons milk
75 g (3 oz) mixed dried fruit
25 g (1 oz) chopped mixed
  candied peel

*Brandy Butter*
100 g (4 oz) unsalted butter
grated rind of 1 lemon
100 g (4 oz) caster sugar
2 tablespoons brandy

# Eve's Pudding

Peel and core the apples. Cut them into pieces and chop coarsely (metal blade). Grease an ovenware dish and put the apples in it. Sprinkle on the brown sugar. Mix the fruit and sugar lightly together. Put the margarine, sugar, flour, eggs, lemon rind and essence into the processor bowl and mix to a soft dough (plastic blade). Spread over the apples. Bake at 180 °C/350 °F/Gas Mark 4 for 40 minutes. Sprinkle with caster sugar and serve at once with cream or custard.

450 g (1 lb) cooking apples
75 g (3 oz) light soft brown
  sugar
100 g (4 oz) soft margarine
100 g (4 oz) caster sugar
100 g (4 oz) self-raising flour
2 eggs
grated rind of 1 lemon
$\frac{1}{4}$ teaspoon vanilla essence
extra caster sugar

# Half Pay Pudding

175 g (6 oz) day-old white
  bread
100 g (4 oz) self-raising flour
100 g (4 oz) shredded suet
pinch of salt
6 tablespoons milk
2 tablespoons golden syrup
100 g (4 oz) currants
100 g (4 oz) seedless raisins

Discard the crusts from the bread and make bread into crumbs (metal blade). Keep on one side. Mix the flour, suet, salt, milk and syrup to a soft dough (plastic blade). Add the breadcrumbs and mix until just incorporated. Stir in the currants and raisins. Grease a pudding basin and put the mixture in it. Grease a piece of greaseproof paper and cover the basin. Cover again with a piece of foil. Put into a saucepan with boiling water to come half-way up the sides of the basin. Cover the pan with a lid and boil for 2 hours, adding more boiling water from time to time so that the pan does not become dry. Turn out and serve with warm golden syrup or custard.

# Golden Pineapple Sponge

25 g (1 oz) butter
2 tablespoons dark soft brown
  sugar
450 g (1 lb) canned pineapple
  rings
6 glacé cherries
100 g (4 oz) soft margarine
100 g (4 oz) caster sugar
2 eggs
100 g (4 oz) self-raising flour

Grease a 900 ml (1½ pint) pie-dish liberally with butter. Sprinkle on the brown sugar. Drain the pineapple rings and arrange 6 rings on the base of the pie-dish. Place a cherry in the centre of each ring. Chop the remaining pineapple coarsely (metal blade) and keep on one side. Mix the margarine and sugar with the eggs and flour until well creamed (plastic blade). Stir in the chopped pineapple and spread over the pineapple rings in the pie-dish. Bake at 180°C/350°F/Gas Mark 4 for 45 minutes. Turn out and serve with custard.

# Baked Orange Pudding

225 g (8 oz) day-old white
  bread
4 oranges
75 g (3 oz) light soft brown
  sugar
2 eggs and 2 egg yolks
4 tablespoons brandy

Discard crusts from the bread and make bread into crumbs (metal blade). Keep on one side. Grate the rind from 2 oranges and mix with the breadcrumbs. Squeeze out all the orange juice (juice extractor). Mix the breadcrumbs, orange juice, sugar, eggs, egg yolks and brandy until well blended (plastic blade). Grease an ovenware dish and put the mixture in it. Bake at 180°C/350°F/Gas Mark 4 for 45 minutes. Serve hot with cream.

# Date Pudding

Discard the crusts from the bread and make bread into crumbs (metal blade). Keep on one side. Cut the dates into chunks, chop them coarsely (metal blade) and mix with the almonds. Mix the suet, breadcrumbs, salt, egg and syrup to a soft dough (plastic blade). Stir in the dates and almonds. Grease a pudding basin and put the mixture in it. Grease a piece of greaseproof paper and cover the basin. Cover again with a piece of foil. Put into a saucepan with boiling water to come half-way up the sides of the basin. Cover the pan with a lid and boil for 2 hours, adding more boiling water from time to time so that the pan does not become dry. Turn out and serve with warm golden syrup or marmalade.

225 g (8 oz) day-old white bread
350 g (12 oz) stoned dates
15 g ($\frac{1}{2}$ oz) blanched almonds
100 g (4 oz) shredded suet
pinch of salt
1 egg
2 tablespoons golden syrup

# Chocolate Bread Pudding

Discard the crusts from the bread and make bread into crumbs (metal blade). Keep on one side. Grate the chocolate (disc A). Put the milk and butter into a pan and bring to the boil. Take off the heat and stir in the grated chocolate until melted. Add the breadcrumbs and then simmer for 10 minutes. Cool this mixture and return it to the processor bowl. Add the sugar, egg yolks and essence. Mix until well blended (plastic blade), then transfer to another bowl. Whisk the egg whites to stiff peaks (whisk attachment) and fold into the chocolate mixture. Thoroughly grease a pudding basin and put the mixture in it. Grease a piece of greaseproof paper and cover the basin. Cover again with a piece of foil. Put into a saucepan with boiling water to come half-way up the sides of the basin. Cover the pan with a lid and boil for 2 hours, adding more boiling water from time to time so that the pan does not become dry. Turn out and serve hot with cream or chocolate sauce (see Profiteroles, page 112).

175 g (6 oz) day-old white bread
100 g (4 oz) plain chocolate
150 ml ($\frac{1}{4}$ pint) milk
75 g (3 oz) butter
100 g (4 oz) caster sugar
2 eggs, separated
$\frac{1}{4}$ teaspoon vanilla essence

# Biscuit Puddings

100 g (4 oz) digestive biscuits
100 g (4 oz) soft margarine
100 g (4 oz) dark soft brown
  sugar
150 ml (¼ pint) creamy milk
2 eggs and 2 egg yolks

Break the biscuits into pieces and make into coarse crumbs (metal blade). Keep on one side. Cream the margarine and sugar (plastic blade). Add the biscuit crumbs, milk, egg and egg yolks. Process until well mixed. Put into 4–6 individual ovenware dishes. Bake at 180°C/350°F/Gas Mark 4 for 25 minutes. Serve with hot raspberry or apricot jam.

# Baked Golden Pudding and Honey Sauce

3 tablespoons clear honey
1 tablespoon water
100 g (4 oz) soft margarine
100 g (4 oz) sugar
2 eggs
100 g (4 oz) self-raising flour
pinch of salt

*Sauce*
1 lemon
100 g (4 oz) clear honey
150 ml (¼ pint) water

Thoroughly grease a pie-dish. In a bowl mix the honey and water and put on the base of the pie-dish. Mix the margarine, sugar, eggs, flour and salt to a soft dough (plastic blade). Put into the pie-dish. Grease a piece of greaseproof paper and cover the pie-dish. Bake at 180°C/350°F/Gas Mark 4 for 45 minutes.

Make the sauce. Grate the lemon rind and squeeze out the juice (juice extractor). Simmer with the honey and water for 10 minutes. Serve the pudding hot with hot sauce.

# Apricot Brown Betty

450 g (1 lb) ripe fresh apricots
225 g (8 oz) wholemeal bread
50 g (2 oz) melted butter
100 g (4 oz) light soft brown
  sugar
½ lemon
½ teaspoon ground cinnamon
150 ml (¼ pint) boiling water

Cut the apricots in half and remove the stones. Chop coarsely (metal blade) and keep on one side. Discard crusts from the bread and make bread into crumbs (metal blade). Mix the crumbs with melted butter. Grease a baking dish and put in half the fruit. Sprinkle with half the sugar. Grate the lemon rind and squeeze out the juice (juice extractor). Sprinkle the fruit with half the rind and juice and half the cinnamon. Top with half the buttered crumbs. Repeat the layers. Pour on the water. Bake at 180°C/350°F/Gas Mark 4 for 45 minutes. Serve with cream or custard.

# Rhubarb Toffee Pudding

Grease a 1·2 litre (2 pint) pudding basin liberally with the butter and sprinkle with the brown sugar. Wash and trim the rhubarb, cut in pieces and chop coarsely (metal blade). Keep rhubarb on one side. Mix flour, salt, suet and cold water to a soft dough (plastic blade). Cut off one-third for a lid. Roll out the remaining dough very lightly and line the pudding basin. Put in half the rhubarb. Grate the rind of the lemon and squeeze out the juice (juice extractor). In a bowl mix the sugar, sultanas, peel, grated rind and juice of the lemon, and the cinnamon. Sprinkle this mixture on to the rhubarb and cover with the remaining rhubarb. Add the water. Cover with the remaining dough. Grease a piece of greaseproof paper and place on top. Bake at 180°C/350°F/Gas Mark 4 for 1¼ hours. Turn out and serve with cream or custard.

25 g (1 oz) butter
50 g (2 oz) light soft brown sugar
675 g (1½ lb) rhubarb
225 g (8 oz) self-raising flour
1 teaspoon salt
75 g (3 oz) shredded suet
150 ml (¼ pint) cold water
½ lemon
100 g (4 oz) sugar
50 g (2 oz) sultanas
25 g (1 oz) chopped mixed candied peel
pinch of ground cinnamon
6 tablespoons water

# Cranberry Meringue Pudding

Peel and core the apples and cut them into pieces. Chop coarsely (metal blade). Wipe the cranberries and add to the apples. Continue processing until the cranberries are chopped. Put into a pan and simmer until the fruit is soft. Make the spongecake into crumbs (metal blade). Stir into fruit, add granulated sugar. Leave until cool. Stir egg yolks into the mixture. Grease an ovenware dish and put the mixture in it. Bake at 180°C/350°F/Gas Mark 4 for 25 minutes until the top is set. Whisk the egg whites to stiff peaks (whisk attachment). With the motor running, add half the caster sugar through the feeder tube and process for 20 seconds. Fold in the remaining sugar with a metal spoon. Spoon the meringue mixture on top of the pudding. Continue baking for 10 minutes. Serve very hot with vanilla ice cream.

450 g (1 lb) cooking apples
225 g (8 oz) fresh cranberries
75 g (3 oz) stale spongecake
100 g (4 oz) granulated sugar
2 eggs, separated
100 g (4 oz) caster sugar

# Apple and Mincemeat Charlotte

8 medium slices white bread
  (small loaf)
75 g (3 oz) shredded suet
75 g (3 oz) light soft brown
  sugar
1 teaspoon ground cinnamon
450 g (1 lb) cooking apples
225 g (8 oz) fruit mincemeat
1 lemon

Discard the crusts from the bread and make bread into crumbs (metal blade). Mix the breadcrumbs with the suet, sugar and cinnamon. Peel and core the apples and grate them (disc C). Mix the grated apples with the mincemeat. Grate the lemon rind. Squeeze juice from lemon (juice extractor) and mix the rind and juice with the mincemeat. Divide the breadcrumb mixture into 3. Grease a 1·2 litre (2 pint) round ovenware dish. Sprinkle one-third of the mixture on the base of it. Bake at 200 °C/400 °F/Gas Mark 6 for 10 minutes. Spread on half the apple mixture. Top with another portion of crumb mixture, and then spread on the remaining apples. Sprinkle the top with the remaining breadcrumb mixture. Bake at 200 °C/400 °F/Gas Mark 6 for 40 minutes until crisp and golden. Serve hot with cream or custard.

# Apple Honey Charlotte

50 g (2 oz) butter
150 g (5 oz) day-old white
  bread
450 g (1 lb) cooking apples
100 g (4 oz) honey
1 lemon
1 tablespoon water

Grease a pie-dish thickly with some of the butter and keep the rest on one side. Remove the crusts from the bread and make bread into crumbs (metal blade). Press a layer of crumbs over the bottom and sides of the dish. Peel and core the apples, cut them in quarters and slice (disc D). Arrange alternate layers of apples and crumbs in the dish, finishing with crumbs. Put the honey into a small pan. Grate the rind from the lemon and squeeze out the juice (juice extractor). Add the rind and juice to the honey with the water. Bring to the boil and stir well to mix. Pour over the apples and crumbs. Cut the remaining butter into thin flakes and arrange on top of the crumbs. Bake at 170 °C/325 °F/Gas Mark 3 for 1¼ hours. Serve hot with cream or custard.

# Baked Raisin Pudding

4 thick slices white bread
  (large loaf)
75 g (3 oz) seedless raisins
50 g (2 oz) soft margarine
65 g (2½ oz) sugar
2 eggs
450 ml (¾ pint) milk
grated rind of ½ orange
pinch of salt

Discard the crusts from the bread and make bread into crumbs (metal blade). Put into a bowl and mix with the raisins. Blend the margarine, sugar, eggs, milk, orange rind and salt (blender attachment) for 20 seconds, and pour over the crumb mixture. Stir well. Grease a pie-dish and put mixture in it. Stand the dish in a roasting tin and pour in hot water so that it comes half-way up the dish. Bake at 150 °C/350 °F/Gas Mark 4 for 1 hour. Serve hot with cream or warm marmalade.

# Apricot Crumble

Drain the apricots and reserve the juice. Chop the fruit coarsely (metal blade). Thoroughly grease an ovenware dish and put the fruit in it. Dot with flakes of butter and sprinkle with sugar and cinnamon. Add 3 tablespoons syrup from the can. Mix the butter, sugar, flour and ginger until the mixture is like coarse breadcrumbs (plastic blade). Sprinkle on top of the fruit and press down very lightly with a fork. Bake at 180 °C/350 °F/Gas Mark 4 for 45 minutes. Serve hot with cream or custard.

450 g (1 lb) canned apricots
15 g ($\frac{1}{2}$ oz) butter
50 g (2 oz) light soft brown
  sugar
pinch of ground cinnamon

*Topping*
50 g (2 oz) butter
25 g (1 oz) light soft brown
  sugar
75 g (3 oz) plain flour
pinch of ground ginger

# Coffee Walnut Pudding and Coffee Cream Sauce

Chop the walnuts coarsely (metal blade) and keep on one side. Cream the margarine and caster sugar until soft and fluffy (plastic blade). With the motor running, add the eggs one at a time, with a little flour, through the feeder tube. When they are incorporated, switch off the machine. Add the flour, coffee powder and milk and mix just long enough to make a soft dough. Stir in the walnuts. Thoroughly grease a pudding basin and put the mixture in it. Grease a piece of greaseproof paper and cover the basin. Cover again with foil. Put into a saucepan with boiling water to come half-way up the sides of the basin. Cover the pan with a lid and boil for 1$\frac{1}{2}$ hours adding more boiling water from time to time so that the pan does not become dry.

While the pudding is steaming prepare the sauce. Beat the eggs lightly (plastic blade). With the motor running, pour the coffee, sugar and salt through the feeder tube until the mixture is well blended. Pour into the top of a double saucepan, or into a basin over hot water, and cook without boiling until the mixture is thick enough to coat the back of a spoon. Leave until cold. Whip the cream (whisk attachment) to soft peaks. Add the coffee mixture and continue whipping until just mixed. Turn the pudding on to a warm serving plate and serve the cold sauce separately.

50 g (2 oz) walnut halves
100 g (4 oz) soft margarine
100 g (4 oz) caster sugar
2 eggs
175 g (6 oz) self-raising flour
2 teaspoons coffee powder
1 tablespoon milk

*Sauce*
2 eggs
6 tablespoons hot strong coffee
50 g (2 oz) caster sugar
pinch of salt
150 ml ($\frac{1}{4}$ pint) double cream

# Rhubarb Pudding and Brown Sugar Sauce

225 g (8 oz) rhubarb
100 g (4 oz) butter
100 g (4 oz) sugar
225 g (8 oz) self-raising flour
2 eggs
pinch of salt
pinch of ground ginger

*Sauce*
50 g (2 oz) butter
50 g (2 oz) light soft brown
  sugar
4 tablespoons single cream

Wash the rhubarb and cut it into pieces. Chop coarsely (metal blade) and keep on one side. Cream the butter and sugar (plastic blade). Add the flour, eggs, salt and ginger and mix to a soft dough. Add to the rhubarb and stir well to mix. Thoroughly grease a pudding basin and put the mixture in it. Grease a piece of greaseproof paper and cover the basin. Cover again with foil. Put into a pan of boiling water to come half-way up the sides of the basin. Cover the pan with a lid and steam for 1½ hours, adding more water from time to time so that the pan does not become dry.

Just before serving, prepare the sauce. Put the butter into a small pan and melt over low heat. Stir in the sugar and cream over low heat until the sugar has dissolved. Turn the pudding on to a warm serving plate and serve at once with the warm sauce.

# Baked Cherry Batter

450 g (1 lb) ripe black eating
  cherries
3 eggs
100 g (4 oz) plain flour
50 g (2 oz) caster sugar
300 ml (½ pint) milk

Thoroughly grease a 1·2 litre (2 pint) ovenware dish. Stone the cherries and arrange them on the base of the dish. Beat the eggs, flour and sugar until mixed (plastic blade). With the motor running, pour in the milk through the feeder tube and continue processing to make a creamy batter. Pour over the fruit and bake at 190 °C/375 °F/Gas Mark 5 for 45 minutes. Serve at once sprinkled with some extra caster sugar, and with cream or custard.

# Cream Cheese and Apple Flan

225 g (8 oz) made sweet
  shortcrust pastry (page 87)
450 g (1 lb) eating apples
50 g (2 oz) light soft brown
  sugar
1 tablespoon orange
  marmalade
½ teaspoon ground mixed spice
100 g (4 oz) soft cream cheese
150 ml (¼ pint) double cream

Roll out the pastry and line a 20 cm (8 in) flan tin. Bake blind at 200 °C/400 °F/Gas Mark 6 for 25 minutes. Cool and put on to a serving dish. Peel and core the apples. Chop coarsely (metal blade). Put into a pan with the sugar, marmalade and spice and simmer gently until the apples are soft. Cool for 10 minutes, then return to the processor bowl and mix until smooth (plastic blade). Leave until completely cold. Spread the flan case with the cream cheese and place the apple purée on top. Whip the cream to soft peaks (whisk attachment) and spoon on top of the apples. Chill for an hour before serving.

# Basic Cheesecake

Break up the biscuits and make into crumbs (metal blade). Grease a 20 cm (8 in) round cake tin with removable base and line the base with greased greaseproof paper. Sprinkle the crumbs on the base. Mix the cottage cheese, lemon juice and rind, orange rind, cornflour, egg yolks and cream until smooth (plastic blade). Transfer to another bowl. Whisk the egg whites to stiff peaks (whisk attachment). With the motor running, add half the sugar through the feeder tube and process for 20 seconds. Fold in the remaining sugar with a metal spoon. Fold this meringue mixture into the cheese mixture. Pour on top of the biscuits. Bake at 180 °C/350 °F/Gas Mark 4 for 1 hour. Turn off the oven and leave the cheesecake in the oven until cold. Remove from the tin and serve with fresh', canned or frozen fruit.

50 g (2 oz) digestive biscuits
450 g (1 lb) cottage cheese
1 teaspoon lemon juice
1 teaspoon grated lemon rind
1 teaspoon grated orange rind
1 tablespoon cornflour
2 eggs, separated
2 tablespoons double cream
100 g (4 oz) caster sugar

# Old English Cheesecake

Grease a 20 cm (8 in) flan tin. Roll out the pastry and line the tin with it. Prick with a fork and bake at 180 °C/350 °F/Gas Mark 4 for 30 minutes. Leave to cool. Cut the butter into pieces and mix with the curd cheese, sugar, eggs, brandy, cream and spice until smooth (plastic blade). Stir in the raisins. Put into the pastry case. Bake at 170 °C/325 °F/Gas Mark 3 for 40 minutes. Serve cold.

225 g (8 oz) made shortcrust
  pastry (page 86)
50 g (2 oz) butter
350 g (12 oz) soft curd cheese
75 g (3 oz) caster sugar
2 eggs
1 tablespoon brandy
2 tablespoons single cream
pinch of ground mixed spice
50 g (2 oz) seedless raisins

# Honey Cheesecake

Roll out the pastry and line a 20 cm (8 in) pie-plate. Blend the cottage cheese, honey, sugar, butter, eggs and cinnamon until smooth (plastic blade). Put into the pastry case and sprinkle with a topping made of caster sugar and cinnamon mixed together. Bake at 200 °C/400 °F/Gas Mark 6 for 10 minutes and then 190 °C/375 °F/Gas Mark 5 for 30 minutes. Leave until cold before serving.

225 g (8 oz) made sweet
  shortcrust pastry (page 87)
100 g (4 oz) cottage cheese
50 g (2 oz) honey
50 g (2 oz) caster sugar
25 g (1 oz) butter
2 eggs
½ teaspoon ground cinnamon

*Topping*
25 g (1 oz) caster sugar
½ teaspoon ground cinnamon

1. Crushing chocolate digestive biscuits into crumbs

2. Whipping cream to soft peaks

3. Pouring chocolate cream filling on to biscuit base

# Chocolate Chiffon Pie

150 g (5 oz) plain chocolate
  digestive biscuits
100 g (4 oz) butter
100 g (4 oz) sugar

*Filling*
300 ml (½ pint) whipping cream
2 teaspoons gelatine
2 tablespoons water
250 ml (8 fl oz) milk
50 g (2 oz) plain chocolate
3 eggs, separated
100 g (4 oz) sugar
pinch of salt
3 drops vanilla essence

Crush the biscuits into crumbs (metal blade). Melt the butter in a pan and add the sugar and crumbs. Press into base of a 25 cm (10 in) ovenware dish and bake at 180 °C/350 °F/Gas Mark 4 for 15 minutes. Cool at room temperature and then chill in the refrigerator until firm.

To make the filling, whip the cream to soft peaks and keep on one side (whisk attachment). Mix the gelatine and water in a small bowl or cup and put the bowl into a pan of hot water, stirring until the mixture is syrupy. Heat the milk and chocolate together until just below boiling point. Mix the egg yolks (plastic blade). Start the machine and pour in the sugar, salt and essence through the feeder tube and gradually pour in the milk mixture. When eggs and milk are combined, return to the saucepan and cook very gently until the mixture thickens like custard. Remove from heat and cool for 10 .minutes, then stir in the gelatine. Leave until thick and cool. Mix with the cream just long enough to blend together (plastic blade), then turn into another bowl. Whisk the egg whites to stiff peaks (whisk attachment). Fold into the cream mixture and pour on to the biscuit base. Chill before serving. If liked, decorate with some grated plain chocolate, or with whirls of whipped cream and grated chocolate.

# Fudge Pie

150 g (5 oz) plain chocolate
    digestive biscuits
100 g (4 oz) butter
100 g (4 oz) sugar

*Filling*
100 g (4 oz) walnut halves
100 g (4 oz) marshmallows
225 g (8 oz) butter
150 g (5 oz) caster sugar
50 g (2 oz) plain chocolate
½ teaspoon vanilla essence
2 eggs

Crush the biscuits into crumbs (metal blade). Melt the butter and add the sugar and crumbs. Press into a 25 cm (9 in) pie-plate and bake at 180 °C/350 °F/Gas Mark 4 for 15 minutes. Cool at room temperature and then chill in the refrigerator until firm.

To make the filling, chop the walnuts coarsely (metal blade) and keep on one side. Chop the marshmallows into small pieces (metal blade). Cream the butter and sugar until light and fluffy (plastic blade). Melt the chocolate with the essence in a pan and add to the creamed mixture with the eggs. Continue processing until creamy. Fold in nuts and marshmallows and put into the crumb case. Chill for 2 hours before serving.

# Peach Shortcake

225 g (8 oz) self-raising flour
½ teaspoon salt
pinch of ground nutmeg
25 g (1 oz) caster sugar
50 g (2 oz) soft margarine
150 ml (¼ pint) milk

*Filling and Topping*
50 g (2 oz) softened butter
450 g (1 lb) canned peach slices
150 ml (¼ pint) double cream

Grease a 20 cm (8 in) sandwich tin. Put flour, salt, nutmeg and sugar into the bowl and add margarine. Pour in milk and mix to a soft dough (plastic blade). Divide the dough into 2 pieces and roll out lightly to fit the tin. Put in 1 piece of dough and brush lightly with a little of the softened butter. Put the other piece of dough on top. Bake at 230 °C/450 °F/Gas Mark 8 for 12 minutes. Turn on to a wire rack. Carefully split the layers and put the bottom half on to a serving plate.

Spread each half with softened butter. Drain the peach halves and arrange two-thirds of them on the bottom layer. Top with the second layer. Whip the cream to soft peaks (whisk attachment) and spoon over the top of the shortcake. Decorate with the remaining peach slices. Serve while freshly baked.

# Meringues

Line a baking sheet with a piece of Bakewell parchment. Put the egg whites into the bowl. Fit the lid, but leave out the pusher from the feeder tube. Whisk the egg whites until stiff (whisk attachment) when the whisk will leave track marks as it moves. This will take about 45 seconds, and it is best to process in 15-second stages. With the motor running, pour half the sugar through the feeder tube and process for 20 seconds. Fold in the remaining sugar with a metal spoon. Spoon out the mixture, or pipe it into 16 rounded heaps on the lined baking sheet. Bake at 130°C/250°F/Gas Mark ½ for 2 hours. Turn off the oven but leave in the meringues until the oven is cold. Remove from the baking sheet and store in an airtight tin or the freezer until used. To serve, sandwich halves together with whipped cream or ice cream.

3 egg whites
175 g (6 oz) caster sugar

# Paris–Brest

Melt the butter in the water and bring to the boil. Tip in the flour and salt at once and cook gently, stirring all the time for 2 minutes. Cool for 10 minutes. Put into the processor bowl (plastic blade). With the machine running, add the eggs one at a time through the feeder tube, mixing until completely incorporated. Lightly grease a baking sheet. Put the mixture in a piping bag fitted with a large plain nozzle and pipe out a 20 cm (8 in) ring on the baking sheet. Brush the top with a little beaten egg. Chop almonds (metal blade) and crush sugar, sprinkle over surface. Bake at 200°C/400°F/Gas Mark 6 for 35 minutes until light and golden. Cool on a wire rack. Cut the circle through horizontally.

Make the filling by beating the icing sugar and egg yolks (plastic blade). Boil the milk. With the machine running, add the milk, flour and essence through the feeder tube till well blended. Return to the pan and heat gently, stirring well until smooth and creamy. Leave until cold. Whisk the egg whites to stiff peaks (whisk attachment) and fold into the custard.

Fill the gâteau with this mixture and replace the top so that the filling shows all round. Dust the top thickly with some extra icing sugar.

100 g (4 oz) butter
300 ml (½ pint) water
150 g (5 oz) plain flour
pinch of salt
4 eggs
beaten egg for glazing
50 g (2 oz) blanched almonds
25 g (1 oz) sugar cubes
icing sugar for decoration

*Filling*
50 g (2 oz) icing sugar
3 eggs and 2 egg whites
150 ml (¼ pint) milk
25 g (1 oz) plain flour
¼ teaspoon vanilla essence

1. Adding eggs to choux pastry mixture

2. Piping first ring of choux buns on to shortcrust round

3. Fixing remaining choux buns on to gâteau

# Gâteau St. Honoré

½ quantity made sweet
   shortcrust pastry (page 87)
100 g (4 oz) butter
300 ml (½ pint) water
150 g (5 oz) plain flour
pinch of salt
4 eggs

*Filling and Topping*
300 ml (½ pint) double cream
4 tablespoons caster sugar
crystallised violets or roses

Roll out shortcrust pastry into a 20 cm (8 in) round. Grease a baking sheet and place pastry on it. Prick well with a fork.

Make the choux pastry next. Put the butter and water into a pan and bring to the boil. Tip in the flour and salt and beat with a wooden spoon. Cook gently, stirring all the time for 2 minutes until the mixture leaves the sides of the pan. Cool for 10 minutes. Put into the bowl (plastic blade) and switch on the machine. Add the eggs one at a time through the feeder tube, mixing for 1 minute until completely incorporated. Put the choux pastry into a piping bag fitted with a 1 cm (½ in) plain nozzle. Damp the outside edge of the pastry round and pipe half the choux pastry in adjoining buns round this damp edge. Lightly grease another baking sheet and pipe out the remaining choux pastry in separate buns the same size as the others. Put the choux/shortcrust ring on the top shelf of the oven, and the separate choux buns on the middle shelf. Bake at 200 °C/400 °F/Gas Mark 6 for 30 minutes. Cool on a wire rack. Make a small slit in each of the choux buns to allow steam to escape.

Put the cream and 1 tablespoon sugar into the bowl and whisk to soft peaks (whisk attachment). Fill a piping bag and use some of the cream to fill the choux buns. Put the remaining sugar into a small heavy-based saucepan and heat gently until golden and syrupy. Dip the bases of the separate choux buns in this caramel and fix round the top of the choux ring. Trickle any remaining caramel on top of the puffs and decorate at once with crystallised violets or roses. Pipe the remaining cream in the centre of the gâteau and decorate with more violets or roses.

# Profiteroles with Chocolate Sauce

50 g (2 oz) butter
150 ml (¼ pint) water
65 g (2½ oz) plain flour
pinch of salt
2 eggs
150 ml (¼ pint) double cream

*Sauce*
100 g (4 oz) plain chocolate
225 g (8 oz) sugar
150 ml (¼ pint) hot coffee
pinch of salt
½ teaspoon vanilla essence

Put the butter and water in a pan and bring to the boil. Tip in all the flour and salt at once and cook over low heat, stirring well for 2 minutes. Cool for 10 minutes, then put into the bowl (plastic blade). With the machine running, add the eggs one at a time through the feeder tube, mixing until completely incorporated. Lightly grease a baking sheet and put teaspoons of the mixture on it. Bake at 200 °C/400 °F/Gas Mark 6 for 20 minutes. Cool on a wire rack. Whip the cream to soft peaks (whisk attachment) and fill the profiteroles. Pile into a serving dish.

To make the sauce, chop the chocolate finely (metal blade). Blend all the sauce ingredients until smooth (blender attachment). Serve the sauce hot or cold over the profiteroles. The sauce may be made in advance and stored in a covered jar in the refrigerator.

# Victorian Chocolate Shape

450 g (1 lb) day-old white
  bread
600 ml (1 pint) milk
50 g (2 oz) dark soft brown
  sugar
50 g (2 oz) plain chocolate

Discard the crusts and break the bread into pieces. Make into crumbs (metal blade). Put into a bowl with the milk and sugar and leave to soak for 15 minutes. Grate the chocolate (disc A) and stir into the mixture. Grease a pudding basin and put the mixture in it. Grease a piece of greaseproof paper and cover the basin. Cover again with a piece of foil. Put into a saucepan with boiling water to come half-way up the sides of the basin. Cover the pan with a lid and boil for 2 hours, adding more boiling water from time to time so that the pan does not become dry. Leave until cold before turning out. Serve with custard or chocolate sauce (see Profiteroles, above), or with ice cream.

# Fresh Fruit Fool

Wash and hull the berries. Mix to a purée with the sugar, orange rind and lemon juice (metal blade). Put the purée through a sieve to get rid of any pips. Whip the cream to soft peaks (whisk attachment). With the machine running, pour in the fruit purée through feeder tube until the cream and fruit are just mixed. Spoon into tall glasses and chill for an hour before serving. The fool may be decorated with a whirl of whipped cream topped with a piece of fresh fruit.

225 g (8 oz) fresh raspberries, strawberries or blackberries
75 g (3 oz) caster sugar
grated rind of ½ orange
1 teaspoon lemon juice
150 ml (¼ pint) double cream

# Lemon Mousse

Put the water into a pan. Grate the rind of 1 lemon and squeeze the juice from all 3 (juice extractor). Add to the pan with the sugar. Bring to the boil, stirring well, and boil for 5 minutes. Mix the egg yolks until well blended (plastic blade). With the machine running, pour the hot syrup through the feeder tube on to the egg yolks and process until the mixture is light and fluffy. Put the gelatine into a cup with 4 tablespoons water and stand in a pan of hot water. Heat until the gelatine is syrupy. Add to the egg mixture and process just enough to mix. Pour into a bowl and cool until the mixture is just beginning to set. Whip the cream to soft peaks (whisk attachment). Whisk the egg whites to stiff peaks (whisk attachment). Fold the cream and then the egg whites into the lemon mixture. Pour into a serving bowl and chill.

150 ml (¼ pint) water
3 lemons
225 g (8 oz) sugar
4 eggs, separated
15 g (½ oz) gelatine
300 ml (½ pint) double cream

# Frozen Orange Pudding

Break the macaroons into pieces and make into coarse crumbs (metal blade). Sprinkle half the crumbs in an ice-making tray and reserve the rest. Squeeze out the orange and lemon juice (juice extractor). Beat the juices, egg yolks, sugar and salt until well mixed (plastic blade). Pour into the top of a double saucepan or a bowl over boiling water, and cook until thick and creamy. Leave until cool. Whip the cream to soft peaks (whisk attachment). Whisk the egg whites to stiff peaks (whisk attachment). Fold cream and then egg whites into the orange mixture. Pour on top of the macaroon crumbs. Top with the remaining crumbs. Freeze in the ice-making compartment of a refrigerator at lowest setting for 4 hours. Put into the main part of the refrigerator for 1 hour before serving. Turn on to a serving dish and cut into thick slices.

12 macaroons
1 orange
1 lemon
3 eggs, separated
100 g (4 oz) sugar
pinch of salt
300 ml (½ pint) double cream

1. Bread ready for making into crumbs

2. Whipping single cream into double cream

3. Blending apricots, syrup and marmalade to make a sauce

# Brown Bread Ice Cream and Apricot Sauce

100 g (4 oz) day-old brown
    bread
300 ml (½ pint) double cream
150 ml (¼ pint) single cream
75 g (3 oz) icing sugar
1 tablespoon rum
2 eggs, separated

*Apricot Sauce*
450 g (1 lb) canned apricots
4 tablespoons dark chunky
    marmalade

Discard crusts and cut the bread into pieces. Make into crumbs (metal blade). Spread the crumbs on a baking sheet, and bake at 150 °C/300 °F/Gas Mark 2 for 10 minutes. Leave until cold. Whip double cream until just stiff (whisk attachment) and gradually pour in single cream through feeder tube and continue whipping to soft peaks. Exchange whisk for plastic blade. Add icing sugar, rum and egg yolks and mix for 10 seconds (plastic blade). Add crumbs and mix for 5 seconds. Turn into another bowl. Whisk the egg whites to soft peaks (whisk attachment) and fold into the mixture. Pour into an ice tray and freeze in ice compartment of the refrigerator at lowest setting for 3 hours. This ice cream does not need beating while freezing.

Prepare the sauce by blending the apricots, syrup and marmalade until smooth (blender attachment or metal blade). Chill the sauce while the ice cream is freezing. Spoon ice cream into glasses and serve with sauce. Raspberry sauce is equally good with this ice cream.

*Raspberry Sauce*
Combine 450 g (1 lb) fresh or frozen raspberries, 50 g (2 oz) sugar, 4 tablespoons blackcurrant syrup, 4 tablespoons water in a pan and heat gently until juice runs. Purée in blender attachment and then sieve. Chill and serve with ice cream.

# Basic Custard Ice Cream

450 ml (¾ pint) milk
1 vanilla pod
2 egg yolks
50 g (2 oz) caster sugar
pinch of salt
150 ml (¼ pint) double cream

Put the milk into a pan with the vanilla pod. Heat gently until the milk comes to boiling point. Take out the vanilla pod. Cool the milk slightly and then thoroughly blend with the egg yolks, sugar and salt (plastic blade). Pour into the top of a double saucepan or into a bowl over hot water and heat, stirring constantly, until the mixture is of a coating consistency. Leave to cool. Whip the cream to soft peaks (whisk attachment). Fold into custard. Pour into a freezer tray and freeze in the ice-making compartment of the refrigerator at lowest setting for 1 hour. Scoop out the half-frozen mixture into the processor, and mix until smooth (metal blade). Return to the freezer tray and freeze for 1 hour. Scoop out again and mix in the processor until smooth. Return to the freezer tray and freeze for 1 hour. This makes a basic vanilla ice cream.

*Chocolate Ice Cream*
Melt 50 g (2 oz) plain chocolate in 4 tablespoons hot water and add to the vanilla-flavoured milk before mixing with the egg yolks.

*Coffee Ice Cream*
Omit vanilla. Add 1 tablespoon instant coffee powder to the milk as it is heated before mixing with the eggs.

*Tutti Frutti Ice Cream*
Add 75 g (3 oz) mixed dried fruit, 25 g (1 oz) chopped mixed candied peel and 25 g (1 oz) chopped nuts to vanilla ice before freezing.

# Quick Fruit Ice Cream

300 g (10 oz) prepared fruit
100 g (4 oz) caster sugar
150 ml (¼ pint) double cream

Suitable fruit for this ice cream are strawberries, raspberries, blackcurrants, apricots, peaches, bananas, cherries or pineapple. Weigh the fruit after removing skins and stones where necessary. Cut the fruit into pieces and mix with the sugar until the fruit is finely chopped (metal blade). Add the cream and continue mixing until smooth. Pour into a freezing tray and freeze in the ice-making compartment of the refrigerator at lowest setting for 2–3 hours until firm.

# 10. Bread, Cakes, Biscuits and Icings

The food processor is invaluable to those who find bread-making heavy work. The yeast is mixed evenly through the dough by the plastic blade and the machine saves tiring kneading. In addition to kneading (the first mixing process) the machine may also be used for knocking back (the second mixing stage).

The machine only handles enough dough for a 450 g (1 lb) loaf tin using 225 g (8 oz) flour – but the process is so quick and simple that it is possible to make 3 or 4 batches of dough in a few minutes, and this may be made into differently shaped loaves, rolls, yeast cakes and buns.

The slow speed of the food processor used with the plastic blade is ideally suited for the basic rubbing in and creaming actions in cake and biscuit making. Cakes made by the 'creaming' method are best made as one-step cakes, using soft margarine and putting all the ingredients into the processor at once. The 'rubbed-in' method may also be used as the processor can rub fat into dry ingredients, and then liquids are introduced through the feeder tube while the machine is running. Whisked sponges cannot be made in the processor. Choux pastry however is excellent: éclairs, choux buns and elaborate gâteaux may be easily made with exceptionally light and crisp results.

The plastic blade may also be used for making light, fluffy icings. The cutting discs and metal blade may be used for grating or chopping ingredients, and the whisk attachment for whipping cream to give cakes a professional finish.

1. Adding yeast liquid to flour mixture

2. Putting dough into an oiled polythene bag

3. Shaping dough into a plait

# Basic White Bread

7 g ($\frac{1}{4}$ oz) fresh yeast *or* 1
  teaspoon dried yeast
$\frac{1}{2}$ teaspoon sugar
150 ml ($\frac{1}{4}$ pint) warm water
225 g (8 oz) strong plain flour
1 teaspoon salt
15 g ($\frac{1}{2}$ oz) lard
poppy, caraway or sesame
  seeds, optional

Cream the fresh yeast with sugar and stir in the water. If using dried yeast, sprinkle yeast on the water, stir in sugar and leave for 10 minutes until frothy. Mix flour, salt and lard (plastic blade). Add yeast liquid and mix for 1 minute. Yeast may also be added through feeder tube, with machine running. Flour your hands lightly and shape the dough into a ball. Oil a polythene bag and put the dough in it. Leave in a warm place for about 1 hour until the dough has doubled in size. Return the dough to the mixer bowl and mix for 1 minute (plastic blade). Shape the dough into required shape and return to the oiled polythene bag. Leave to prove for 40 minutes. Remove from the bag. Sprinkle with poppy, caraway or sesame seeds, if you wish, and bake at 220 °C/425 °F/Gas Mark 7 for 30 minutes. Cool on a wire rack.

*Brown Bread*
Substitute half the white flour with wholemeal flour.

## To shape bread

### Plait

After the dough has risen, divide into 3 pieces. Lightly roll with the hands on a floured board to form 3 cylinders about 30 cm (12 in) long. Pinch the ends of these cylinders together at one end and plait them together. Pinch the other ends after plaiting. Tuck the ends underneath to keep them firm and give a rounded end to the plait. The dough is now ready for proving.

### Crown

After the dough has risen, divide it into 7 pieces, kneading each one into a ball. Grease a 20 cm (8 in) sandwich tin and arrange 6 balls around the edge. Place the last ball in the centre. After proving, the balls will have joined together to form a 'crown'. This is a useful shape for serving as each person has one section of the loaf, which is like an individual roll.

### Dinner Rolls

After the dough has risen, divide into 8 pieces, kneading each one into a ball. Grease a baking sheet and place the dough on it. Prove as for loaves. Bake at 220 °C/425 °F/Gas Mark 7 for 15 minutes.

### Muffins

Make up recipe with white flour. After the dough has risen, roll out on a floured board 1 cm ($\frac{1}{2}$ in) thick. Leave to rest for 5 minutes covered with polythene and cut out 9 cm ($3\frac{1}{2}$ in) rounds. Placed on a well-floured baking sheet and dust tops with flour or fine semolina. Oil a polythene bag and put the dough in it. Leave for 40 minutes in a warm place. Cook on a hot greased griddle or heavy-based frying pan for 6 minutes each side until golden brown. Alternatively, bake at 230 °C/450 °F/Gas Mark 8 for 10 minutes, turning over muffins after 5 minutes. To serve, pull muffins open all the way round with the fingers, leaving the halves joined in the middle. Toast slowly on both sides. Pull apart, butter each half well, put together again and serve hot.

# Sticky Malt Loaf

If using fresh yeast, mix with the sugar. Heat the water to lukewarm and add the creamed yeast, or sprinkle on the dried yeast with the sugar. Leave in a warm place for 10 minutes until the liquid is frothy. Put the flour and salt into the processor bowl. Heat the malt extract, treacle and butter together until the fat has just melted. With the machine running, pour the yeast liquid through the feeder tube and then the malt liquid and process to a soft dough (plastic blade). Stir in fruit. Shape into a ball. Oil a polythene bag and put the dough in it. Leave for 45 minutes in a warm place until doubled in size. Knead lightly and shape into a cylinder. Grease a 450 g (1 lb) loaf tin. Put the tin into the oiled bag and leave until the dough reaches the top of the tin. Remove bag and bake loaf at 200 °C/400 °F/Gas Mark 6 for 45 minutes. Turn on to a wire rack and brush all over with a wet pastry brush dipped in honey. Leave until cold. Serve sliced and buttered.

15 g (½ oz) fresh yeast *or* 7 g (¼ oz) dried yeast
1 teaspoon sugar
100 ml (4 fl oz) water
225 g (8 oz) strong plain flour
pinch of salt
3 tablespoons malt extract
1 tablespoon black treacle
25 g (1 oz) butter
100 g (4 oz) sultanas
1 tablespoon clear honey

# Mincemeat Doughnuts

If using fresh yeast, mix with the sugar. Heat the cider to lukewarm and add the creamed yeast, or sprinkle on the dried yeast with the sugar. Leave in a warm place for 10 minutes until the liquid is frothy. Cut the margarine into pieces. Mix the flour, salt and margarine just long enough to break up the margarine and mix with the flour (plastic blade). With the machine running, pour the yeast liquid through the feeder tube and mix to a soft dough. Shape the dough into a ball. Oil a polythene bag and put the dough in it. Leave in a warm place for about 45 minutes until the dough has doubled in size. Divide the dough into 12 pieces and knead each one lightly into a ball. Make a deep hole in each and put ½ teaspoon mincemeat in each hole. Mould the dough round so that the mincemeat is covered. Grease a baking sheet, put the dough balls on it and return to the polythene bag. Leave in a warm place for 15 minutes. Remove from the bag. Fry doughnuts in hot deep fat or oil for 10 minutes, turning occasionally until golden brown. Drain on kitchen paper. Mix sugar and cinnamon and roll hot doughnuts in this mixture until completely coated. Eat while fresh.

15 g (½ oz) fresh yeast *or* 7 g (¼ oz) dried yeast
1 teaspoon sugar
150 ml (¼ pint) cider
225 g (8 oz) strong plain flour
pinch of salt
25 g (1 oz) block margarine
2 tablespoons fruit mincemeat
fat or oil for deep frying
100 g (4 oz) caster sugar
½ teaspoon ground cinnamon

# Rich Fruit Buns

7 g ($\frac{1}{4}$ oz) fresh yeast *or* 1
    teaspoon dried yeast
25 g (1 oz) caster sugar
5 tablespoons milk
225 g (8 oz) strong plain flour
pinch of salt
pinch of ground mixed spice
25 g (1 oz) butter
1 egg
75 g (3 oz) mixed dried fruit

*Glaze*
25 g (1 oz) sugar
4 tablespoons water

If using fresh yeast, mix with 1 teaspoon of the sugar. Heat the milk to lukewarm and add the creamed yeast, or sprinkle on the dried yeast with 1 teaspoon sugar. Leave in a warm place for 10 minutes until the liquid is frothy. Put the flour, salt, spice and remaining sugar into processor bowl. Cut butter into pieces and add to bowl. Process until just mixed (plastic blade). With machine running, pour the liquid through the feeder tube and process to a soft dough. Add egg and process until just mixed. Stir in the dried fruit. Shape the dough into a ball. Grease a polythene bag and put the dough in it. Leave in a warm place for about 1 hour until the dough has doubled in size. Divide the dough into 10 pieces and knead each one lightly into a ball. Grease a baking sheet, place dough balls on it and return to the oiled bag. Leave in a warm place to prove for 15 minutes. Remove bag and bake buns at 220 °C/425 °F/Gas Mark 7 for 15 minutes. Put on to a wire rack.

For the glaze, put the sugar and water into a small pan, stir until dissolved and boil for 3 minutes. Brush the glaze on to the hot buns.

# Devonshire Splits

7 g ($\frac{1}{4}$ oz) fresh yeast *or* 1
    teaspoon dried yeast
15 g ($\frac{1}{2}$ oz) sugar
150 ml ($\frac{1}{4}$ pint) milk
225 g (8 oz) strong plain flour
pinch of salt
25 g (1 oz) butter
75 g (3 oz) strawberry jam
300 ml ($\frac{1}{2}$ pint) double cream
icing sugar

If using fresh yeast, mix with 1 teaspoon of the sugar. Heat the milk with the remaining sugar until lukewarm. Add the creamed yeast, or sprinkle on the dried yeast. Leave for 10 minutes in a warm place until the liquid is frothy. Mix the flour, salt and butter until the butter is incorporated (plastic blade). With the machine running, pour the liquid through the feeder tube and process to a soft dough. Shape the dough into a ball. Oil a polythene bag and put the dough into it. Leave in a warm place for about 1 hour until the dough has doubled in size. Turn on to a lightly floured board, divide into 16 even-sized pieces and knead each one lightly into a ball. Grease a baking sheet, place the dough balls on it and flatten slightly. Return to the oiled bag and leave to prove for 20 minutes. Remove bag and bake buns at 220 °C/425 °F/Gas Mark 7 for 15–20 minutes until golden. Leave to cool on a wire rack. Make a slit in each bun diagonally and spread each side of slit with jam. Whip the cream to firm peaks (whisk attachment) and fill the slits. Dust the tops with sieved icing sugar.

# Scones

Put the flour and salt into the processor bowl. Cut the margarine into small pieces and add to the bowl. Process until the mixture is like fine breadcrumbs (plastic blade). Add the sugar. With the machine running, pour 5 tablespoons of milk gradually through the feeder tube to make a soft dough. Knead the dough lightly on a floured board for 1 minute. Roll out 2 cm (¾ in) thick. Cut out 12 rounds using a 5 cm (2 in) cutter. Grease a baking sheet and put the rounds on it so that they just touch each other. Brush the tops with the remaining milk. Bake at 220 °C/425 °F/Gas Mark 7 for 12 minutes. Cool on a wire rack.

225 g (8 oz) self-raising flour
pinch of salt
50 g (2 oz) block margarine
25 g (1 oz) caster sugar
6 tablespoons milk

*Fruit Scones*
Stir in 50 g (2 oz) mixed dried fruit before rolling out.

*Cheese Scones*
Omit sugar. Add 50 g (2 oz) grated or chopped Cheddar cheese with the milk.

*Cheese and Onion Scones*
Add 1 finely chopped small onion with the cheese and milk. A pinch of dried mixed herbs may also be added.

# Cheese Wheels

Grate the cheese (disc A) and keep on one side. Peel and chop the onion finely (metal blade) and keep on one side. Put the flour, salt and pepper into the processor bowl. Cut the margarine into small cubes and add to the bowl. Process until the mixture looks like coarse breadcrumbs (plastic blade). With the machine running, add the egg and milk through the feeder tube to make a soft dough. Add half the cheese and mix just long enough to incorporate. Put the dough on to a floured surface and roll into a rectangle 18 × 36 cm (7 × 14 in). Spread with tomato purée and then mustard. Sprinkle with onion and the remaining cheese. Roll up lengthways like a Swiss roll. Grease a baking sheet. Cut the dough into 16 slices and place on the sheet. Bake at 220 °C/425 °F/Gas Mark 7 for 20 minutes. Cool on a wire rack.

50 g (2 oz) Cheddar cheese
1 onion
225 g (8 oz) self-raising flour
salt and pepper
50 g (2 oz) block margarine
1 egg
4 tablespoons milk
3 tablespoons tomato purée
2 tablespoons French mustard

# Hot Cheese Loaves

50 g (2 oz) Cheddar cheese
225 g (8 oz) plain flour
1½ teaspoons baking powder
¼ teaspoon salt
50 g (2 oz) block margarine
6 tablespoons milk
pinch of dried mixed herbs

Grate the cheese (disc A) and keep on one side. Put the flour, baking powder and salt into the processor bowl. Cut the margarine into small pieces and add to the bowl. Process until the mixture is like coarse breadcrumbs (plastic blade). With the machine running, pour the milk gradually through the feeder tube and mix to a soft dough. Add the herbs and cheese and mix until just blended. Grease a baking sheet. Form the dough into 2 round cakes and place on the sheet. Flatten slightly and mark each circle deeply in a cross with a knife. Bake at 230 °C/450 °F/Gas Mark 8 for 15 minutes. Cut each circle into 4 wedges. Split each one through, spread with butter and serve hot. This cheese bread makes a good accompaniment to a salad meal.

# Cheese and Celery Teabread

2 celery sticks
50 g (2 oz) walnut halves
225 g (8 oz) cottage cheese
100 g (4 oz) light soft brown
  sugar
225 g (8 oz) self-raising flour
1 teaspoon baking powder
3 eggs

Wash and trim the celery. Chop it finely (metal blade) and keep on one side. Chop the walnuts coarsely (metal blade) and keep on one side. Cream the cottage cheese and sugar until light and fluffy (plastic blade). Add the flour, baking powder and eggs and continue processing to make a soft dough. Grease and line a 450 g (1 lb) loaf tin and bake at 180 °C/350 °F/Gas Mark 4 for 1 hour. Leave in the tin for 5 minutes, then turn out on a wire rack to cool. Serve sliced and buttered.

# Nutty Cheese Loaf

100 g (4 oz) Cheddar cheese
25 g (1 oz) walnut halves
225 g (8 oz) self-raising flour
1 teaspoon salt
1 teaspoon mustard powder
pinch of pepper
pinch of dried mixed herbs
75 g (3 oz) block margarine
2 eggs
150 ml (¼ pint) milk

Grate the cheese (disc A) and keep on one side. Chop the walnuts finely (metal blade), and keep on one side. Put the flour, salt, mustard, pepper and mixed herbs into the processor bowl. Cut the margarine into small pieces and add to the flour. Process until the mixture is like fine breadcrumbs (plastic blade). Mix the eggs and milk together. With the machine running, pour the liquid gradually through the feeder tube to make a soft dough. Add the cheese and walnuts and mix just long enough to incorporate. Grease a 450 g (1 lb) loaf tin and put the mixture in it. Bake at 180 °C/350 °F/Gas Mark 4 for 1 hour. Turn out and cool on a wire rack. Serve sliced and buttered.

# Banana Bread

Peel the bananas and cut them into pieces. Chop until they are a purée (metal blade) and keep on one side. Mix the flour, baking powder, salt, margarine, sugar and lemon rind until well blended (plastic blade). In a bowl mix the egg and 3 tablespoons milk together. With the machine running, pour gradually through the feeder tube to make a soft batter. If necessary add a little more milk. Grease and flour a 450 g (1 lb) loaf tin and put the mixture in it. Bake at 190 °C/375 °F/Gas Mark 5 for 45 minutes. Turn out and cool on a wire rack. Serve sliced and buttered.

3 ripe bananas
225 g (8 oz) plain flour
3 teaspoons baking powder
pinch of salt
50 g (2 oz) soft margarine
50 g (2 oz) light soft brown sugar
grated rind of 1 lemon
1 egg
3–4 tablespoons milk

# Treacle Raisin Loaf

Chop the nuts finely (metal blade). Put the flours and sugar into the processor bowl. Heat together the black treacle and milk until lukewarm. Stir in the soda. With the motor running, pour the mixture through the feeder tube until well blended (plastic blade). Add the egg and mix to a firm dough. Stir in the chopped nuts and raisins. Grease a 450 g (1 lb) loaf tin and put the mixture in it. Bake at 180 °C/350 °F/Gas Mark 4 for 1 hour. Turn on to a wire rack to cool. Serve sliced and buttered.

25 g (1 oz) mixed nuts
100 g (4 oz) plain flour
100 g (4 oz) plain wholemeal flour
50 g (2 oz) granulated sugar
75 g (3 oz) black treacle
150 ml ($\frac{1}{4}$ pint) milk
1 teaspoon bicarbonate of soda
1 small egg
75 g (3 oz) seedless raisins

# Peanut Butter Loaf

Chop the peanuts coarsely (metal blade) and keep on one side. Cream the sugar and peanut butter until light and fluffy (plastic blade). Add the flour and salt and mix until just blended. With the machine running, gradually add the egg and milk through the feeder tube and mix to a soft dough. Stir in peanuts. Grease a 450 g (1 lb) loaf tin and put the mixture in it. Bake at 190 °C/375 °F/Gas Mark 5 for 45 minutes. Turn out and cool on a wire rack. Serve sliced and buttered.

50 g (2 oz) salted peanuts
100 g (4 oz) light soft brown sugar
75 g (3 oz) peanut butter
225 g (8 oz) self-raising flour
pinch of salt
1 small egg
150 ml ($\frac{1}{4}$ pint) milk

1. Dates ready for chopping

2. Margarine and sugar ready to be creamed

3. Adding chopped dates and walnuts to cake mixture

# Date and Walnut Cake

50 g (2 oz) walnut halves
225 g (8 oz) stoned dates
175 g (6 oz) soft margarine
175 g (6 oz) light soft brown
  sugar
225 g (8 oz) plain flour
1½ teaspoons baking powder
3 eggs
2 tablespoons milk
3 tablespoons icing sugar

Chop the walnuts coarsely (metal blade). Chop the dates finely (metal blade). Keep the dates and walnuts on one side. Cream the margarine and sugar until light and fluffy (plastic blade). Sieve together the flour and baking powder. Add the eggs one at a time with a little of the flour and milk through the feeder tube, mixing for 10 seconds after each addition. Add the remaining flour and mix just long enough for the flour to be incorporated. Stir in the dates and nuts. Grease a 1 kg (2 lb) loaf tin and put the mixture in it. Bake at 170 °C/325 °F/Gas Mark 3 for 1½ hours. Cool in the tin for 10 minutes, then turn out on to a wire rack to finish cooling. Sieve the icing sugar over the top just before serving.

# Basic Sandwich Cake

175 g (6 oz) self-raising flour
1½ teaspoons baking powder
175 g (6 oz) soft margarine
175 g (6 oz) caster sugar
3 eggs

Sift the flour and baking powder into the processor bowl. Add the remaining ingredients and process until light and fluffy (plastic blade). Grease two 18 cm (7 in) sandwich tins and divide the mixture between them. Bake at 180°C/350°F/Gas Mark 4 for 30 minutes. Cool on a wire rack.

*Jam Sandwich*
Sandwich the cakes together with jam and sprinkle the top with caster sugar or sieved icing sugar.

*Cream Sandwich*
Whip 150 ml (¼ pint) double cream to soft peaks. Spread a little jam on one cake, top with cream and put on the second cake. Sprinkle top with caster or icing sugar. Chopped fresh, canned or frozen fruit may be mixed with the cream.

*Lemon or Orange Sandwich*
Add 1 teaspoon grated lemon or orange rind and 1 tablespoon lemon or orange juice to ingredients. Finish with appropriate butter cream for filling and topping.

*Coffee Sandwich*
Add 1 tablespoon coffee essence to ingredients. Finish with coffee butter cream for filling and topping.

*Chocolate Sandwich*
Add 25 g (1 oz) cocoa and 1 tablespoon milk to ingredients. Finish with chocolate butter cream for filling and topping, and sprinkle on 50 g (2 oz) chopped walnuts.

# Simple Gingerbread

Put the flour, sugar, ginger, spice and soda into the processor bowl and add the eggs and milk. Mix until just blended (plastic blade). Put the treacle, syrup and margarine into a pan and warm together until the margarine has melted. Cool to lukewarm. With the machine running, pour the treacle mixture through the feeder tube and mix until just blended. Grease and line an 18 cm (7 in) square tin and put the mixture in it. Bake at 150 °C/300 °F/Gas Mark 2 for 1½ hours. Cool in the tin for 10 minutes and then turn out on a wire rack to cool. Gingerbread tastes better if kept in a storage tin for a day or two before cutting.

225 g (8 oz) plain flour
50 g (2 oz) dark soft brown sugar
2 teaspoons ground ginger
1 teaspoon ground mixed spice
1 teaspoon bicarbonate of soda
2 eggs
150 ml (¼ pint) milk
175 g (6 oz) black treacle
50 g (2 oz) golden syrup
100 g (4 oz) margarine

# Walnut Gingerbread

Chop the walnuts and crystallised ginger finely (metal blade) and keep on one side. Cream the margarine and sugar together (plastic blade). Add the flour, ground ginger, baking powder, salt, egg and milk, and mix to a very soft dough. Add the chopped walnuts and crystallised ginger and mix until blended. Grease a 450 g (1 lb) loaf tin and put the mixture in it. Sprinkle with demerara sugar. Bake at 180 °C/350 °F/Gas Mark 4 for 1 hour 5 minutes. Cool on a wire rack. Serve sliced and buttered.

75 g (3 oz) walnut halves
25 g (1 oz) crystallised ginger
50 g (2 oz) soft margarine
50 g (2 oz) light soft brown sugar
225 g (8 oz) self-raising flour
2 teaspoons ground ginger
1 teaspoon baking powder
¼ teaspoon salt
1 egg
150 ml (¼ pint) milk
2 teaspoons demerara sugar

# Walnut Spice Cake

Reserve 6 walnut halves for decoration. Chop the rest finely and keep on one side (metal blade). Mix the margarine, sugar and honey until just blended (plastic blade). Add the eggs, flour, baking powder, spice and cinnamon and continue mixing until well mixed. Add the chopped walnuts and mix until blended. Grease a 20 cm (8 in) round cake tin and put the mixture in it. Bake at 180 °C/350 °F/Gas Mark 4 for 45 minutes. Turn on to a wire rack to cool. Mix the icing sugar with enough hot water to give a spreading consistency. Spread on top of the cake and decorate with walnut halves.

100 g (4 oz) walnut halves
150 g (5 oz) soft margarine
50 g (2 oz) light soft brown sugar
3 tablespoons clear honey
2 eggs
175 g (6 oz) self-raising flour
1 teaspoon baking powder
2 teaspoons ground mixed spice
½ teaspoon ground cinnamon
100 g (4 oz) icing sugar

1. Adding egg to creamed butter and sugar

2. Adding chopped apple to cake mixture

3. Spreading butter cream filling on cake

# Dorset Apple Cake

225 g (8 oz) eating apples
100 g (4 oz) butter
100 g (4 oz) sugar
1 egg
225 g (8 oz) plain flour
1½ teaspoons baking powder
pinch of salt
blanched almonds

*Filling*
75 g (3 oz) butter
75 g (3 oz) light soft brown
    sugar

Peel and core the apples. Cut them into quarters and then chop coarsely (metal blade). Keep the apples on one side. Cream the butter and sugar until light and fluffy (plastic blade). Add the egg, and cream the mixture for 10 seconds. Sieve the flour, baking powder and salt together. Add to the creamed mixture and mix for a few seconds until incorporated. Stir in the chopped apple. Grease a 20 cm (8 in) round cake tin and put the mixture in it. Bake at 180 °C/350 °F/Gas Mark 4 for 50 minutes. Turn on to a wire rack to cool. After 10 minutes, split through the cake with a sharp knife.

To make the filling, cream the butter and brown sugar until light and fluffy (plastic blade). Spread half the mixture between the pieces of cake, and use the rest to spread on top. Decorate with almonds. Eat freshly baked.

# Apricot Spice Cake

100 g (4 oz) soft margarine
175 g (6 oz) caster sugar
2 eggs
4 tablespoons hot water
300 g (10 oz) plain flour
1 teaspoon bicarbonate of soda
1 teaspoon ground mixed spice
225 g (8 oz) apricot jam

*Icing*
100 g (4 oz) icing sugar
2 tablespoons orange juice

Mix the margarine and sugar until light and fluffy (plastic blade). With the machine running, add the eggs one at a time through the feeder tube, and then the hot water. Sift together the flour, soda and spice. Add to the mixture with the jam and process until completely blended. Grease a 20 cm (8 in) round cake tin and put the mixture in it. Bake at 180 °C/350 °F/Gas Mark 4 for 1¼ hours. Turn on to a wire rack to cool.

The cake may be finished with icing. Stir together the icing sugar and orange juice and spread over the cake.

# Lemon Yogurt Cake

175 g (6 oz) plain flour
2 teaspoons bicarbonate of soda
½ teaspoon salt
50 g (2 oz) soft margarine
300 g (10 oz) caster sugar
3 eggs, separated
150 ml (¼ pint) natural yogurt
grated rind of 1 lemon

*Icing*
100 g (4 oz) icing sugar
2 tablespoons lemon juice
grated rind of 1 lemon

Mix the flour, soda, salt, margarine, sugar, egg yolks, yogurt and lemon rind until well blended (plastic blade). Turn into another bowl. Whisk the egg whites to soft peaks (whisk attachment) and fold into the mixture. Grease and flour a 20 cm (8 in) round cake tin and put the mixture in it. Bake at 180 °C/350 °F/Gas Mark 4 for 1¼ hours. Turn out and cool on a wire rack.

When the cake is cold, stir together the icing sugar, lemon juice and rind and spread over the cake. Leave for 24 hours before cutting.

# Orange Sugar Cake

Grate the rind from the oranges and keep on one side. Squeeze out the orange juice (juice extractor). Cream the margarine and sugar until soft and fluffy (plastic blade). Add the flour, baking powder, salt, eggs and orange juice and continue mixing until well blended. Grease a 25 cm (10 in) spring-form cake tin and put the mixture in it. Mix the orange rind with the granulated sugar and sprinkle on top of the cake mixture. Bake at 180°C/350°F/Gas Mark 4 for 1¼ hours. Open the tin and leave to cool for 10 minutes. Put on a wire rack until cold.

3 oranges
100 g (4 oz) soft margarine
225 g (8 oz) caster sugar
225 g (8 oz) plain flour
2 teaspoons baking powder
pinch of salt
2 eggs
40 g (1½ oz) granulated sugar

# Pineapple Cream Gâteau

Sift the flour and baking powder into the processor bowl. Add the margarine, sugar and eggs and process until light and fluffy (plastic blade). Grease and base-line two 18 cm (7 in) sponge tins and divide the mixture between them. Bake at 180°C/350°F/Gas Mark 4 for 35 minutes. Turn out and cool on a wire rack. Slice each cake in half horizontally.

To make the filling, drain the pineapple rings and chop half of them coarsely (metal blade). Whip the cream to soft peaks (whisk attachment). Reserve a quarter of the cream and mix the rest with the chopped pineapple and brown sugar. Use this to sandwich the cakes together. Top the cake with the remaining cream and pineapple rings. Chill for 30 minutes before serving.

175 g (6 oz) plain flour
1½ teaspoons baking powder
175 g (6 oz) soft margarine
175 g (6 oz) dark soft brown sugar
3 eggs

*Filling*
450 g (1 lb) canned pineapple rings
300 ml (½ pint) double cream
25 g (1 oz) soft dark brown sugar

# Truffle Cakes

225 g (8 oz) stale cake
25 g (1 oz) cocoa
1 tablespoon rum or brandy
150 ml (¼ pint) syrup from
    canned fruit or diluted
    orange squash
4 tablespoons apricot jam
3 tablespoons water
100 g (4 oz) chocolate
    vermicelli
a little icing sugar

The cake may be a mixture of any leftovers such as spongecake, fruit cake or chocolate cake. Break the cake into pieces and make into crumbs (metal blade). Change to the plastic blade and add the cocoa and rum or brandy. With the machine running, add the syrup or squash slowly through the feeder tube (plastic blade). The mixture should be firm enough to roll easily in the hands, so check the consistency before adding all the liquid and omit a little if necessary. Roll the mixture with the hands into 12 balls. Leave in the refrigerator for 1 hour. Put the apricot jam and water into a small pan and heat together until the jam has melted. Put the chocolate vermicelli on a plate. Using tongs or 2 soup spoons, dip the truffle balls quickly into the jam and roll in the vermicelli. Put into paper cake cases. Leave for 1 hour until firm and sprinkle the tops lightly with a little sieved icing sugar.

# Cup Cakes

50 g (2 oz) soft margarine
50 g (2 oz) caster sugar
1 egg
50 g (2 oz) self-raising flour
1 tablespoon milk
flavouring
75 g (3 oz) icing sugar

Put the margarine, sugar, egg, flour and milk into the processor bowl. Add chosen flavouring (see below), and mix until light and soft (plastic blade). Spoon into 12 paper cases on a baking sheet. Bake at 190 °C/375 °F/Gas Mark 5 for 15 minutes. Cool on a wire rack. Mix icing sugar with chosen flavouring (see below), and add enough hot water to give a spreading consistency. Spread on the cakes and leave until icing is set.

*Orange*
Use a little grated orange rind and substitute orange juice for milk. Mix icing sugar with orange juice.

*Lemon*
Use a little grated lemon rind and substitute lemon juice for milk. Mix icing sugar with lemon juice.

*Coffee*
Flavour basic cake mixture with coffee essence, and add a little coffee essence to the icing.

*Chocolate*
Substitute 15 g (½ oz) cocoa for the same quantity of flour. Add 1 teaspoon cocoa to the icing.

# Chocolate Chip Orange Cakes

Grate the rind from the orange and squeeze out the juice (juice extractor). Chop the chocolate finely (metal blade). Mix the margarine, sugar, egg and flour with the orange rind and juice until light and soft (plastic blade). Stir in the chocolate pieces. Put into 12 paper cases on a baking sheet. Bake at 190°C/375°F/Gas Mark 5 for 15 minutes. Cool on a wire rack.

1 orange
50 g (2 oz) plain chocolate
50 g (2 oz) soft margarine
50 g (2 oz) caster sugar
1 egg
75 g (3 oz) self-raising flour

# Viennese Whirls

Cut the butter and margarine into pieces. Add icing sugar and mix until light and fluffy (plastic blade). Add the flour, cornflour and lemon rind and mix until creamy. Grease a baking sheet. Put the mixture into a piping bag fitted with a star nozzle and pipe 24 whirls on the baking sheet. Cut cherries in half and put a piece in the centre of each cake. Bake at 190°C/375°F/Gas Mark 5 for 15 minutes. Cool on a wire rack. Dust thickly with icing sugar.

100 g (4 oz) butter
100 g (4 oz) block margarine
50 g (2 oz) icing sugar
175 g (6 oz) plain flour
50 g (2 oz) cornflour
grated rind of $\frac{1}{2}$ lemon
12 glacé cherries
sieved icing sugar

# Troop Cake

Break the biscuits into pieces and make into crumbs (metal blade). Put into a bowl. Chop the cherries and walnuts coarsely (metal blade) and add to the crumbs. Cut the butter into small pieces and put into the processor bowl with the sugar, cocoa and syrup. Cream until light and fluffy (plastic blade). Add the crumbs, cherries and nuts and mix until just blended (plastic blade). Stir in the sultanas. Grease an 18 cm (7 in) square tin about 2·5 cm (1 in) deep and press the mixture into it. Chill for 5 hours. Melt the chocolate in a bowl over hot water and pour on top of the cake. Leave until the chocolate has set. Cut into squares and remove from the tin.

225 g (8 oz) sweet biscuits
50 g (2 oz) glacé cherries
50 g (2 oz) walnut halves
100 g (4 oz) butter
25 g (1 oz) sugar
25 g (1 oz) cocoa
1 tablespoon golden syrup
50 g (2 oz) sultanas
100 g (4 oz) plain chocolate

# Choux Buns

100 g (4 oz) butter
300 ml (½ pint) water
150 g (5 oz) plain flour
pinch of salt
4 eggs
300 ml (½ pint) double cream
a little icing sugar

Put the butter and water into a pan and bring to the boil. Tip in all the flour and salt at once and cook gently, stirring well for 2 minutes until the mixture leaves the sides of the pan. Cool for 10 minutes and put into the processor bowl (plastic blade). With the machine running, add the eggs one at a time through the feeder tube, mixing until completely incorporated. Lightly grease a baking sheet. Put 15 heaps of the mixture on to the baking sheet. Bake at 200 °C/400 °F/Gas Mark 6 for 30 minutes. Lift on to a wire rack and cut a small slit in the bottom of each bun with a pointed knife to allow steam to escape. Choux buns made with the processor are very light and crisp and there will be no soft mixture to scrape from the shells as sometimes happens when they are made by hand. Whip the cream until thick enough to pipe (whisk attachment). Pipe the cream into the buns and sprinkle with sifted icing sugar. Alternatively you can spoon on melted chocolate, or glacé icing.

*Eclairs*
Grease baking sheets and pipe mixture with plain 1 cm (½ in) nozzle in 10 cm (4 in) lengths on to them. Proceed as for Choux Buns.

# Maxima Biscuits

100 g (4 oz) block margarine
150 g (5 oz) caster sugar
1 egg yolk
225 g (8 oz) plain flour
flavouring

Cut the margarine into small pieces. Mix all the ingredients, except flavouring, to a firm dough (plastic blade). Add chosen flavouring (see below), and process until just mixed. Grease an 18 × 28 cm (7 × 11 in) tin and press the mixture into it. Bake at 180 °C/350 °F/Gas Mark 4 for 30 minutes. Cool and cut into squares.

*Ginger Biscuits*
Add 1 teaspoon ground ginger and 25 g (1 oz) chopped crystallised ginger.

*Coconut Biscuits*
Use 175 g (6 oz) plain flour and 50 g (2 oz) desiccated coconut with 50 g (2 oz) chopped glacé cherries.

*Almond Biscuits*

Add 1 teaspoon almond essence and 25 g (1 oz) flaked almonds. Press into tin and sprinkle with 25 g (1 oz) flaked almonds before baking.

# Savoury Cocktail Biscuits

Grate the cheese (disc A). Cut the butter into small pieces. Add the flour, salt, pepper, mustard, egg yolk and 3 tablespoons water and mix to a firm dough (plastic blade). If the dough looks dry, add the remaining water and mix again. Place the dough on a floured board and sprinkle with the cheese. Fold over the dough to enclose the cheese and roll thinly. Cut into small shapes with different cutters. Grease a baking sheet and put the shapes on it. Prick them lightly with a fork. Chop the peanuts finely (metal blade) and sprinkle on the biscuits. Bake at 180 °C/350 °F/Gas Mark 4 for 15 minutes until golden. Cool on a wire rack and store in a tin.

25 g (1 oz) Cheddar cheese
75 g (3 oz) butter
225 g (8 oz) plain flour
salt and pepper
1 teaspoon mustard powder
1 egg yolk
3–4 tablespoons water
50 g (2 oz) salted peanuts

# Crumb Fingers

Put the flour into the processor bowl. Cut the fat into small cubes and add to the bowl. Process until the fat is just rubbed in (plastic blade). Add the sugar, lemon rind and ginger and process until the mixture is like fine breadcrumbs. Grease a 20 cm (8 in) square tin and press the mixture into it. Press down very lightly with a fork. Bake at 170 °C/325 °F/Gas Mark 3 for 30 minutes. Leave in tin for 10 minutes and mark into fingers with a sharp knife. Leave until completely cold and cut into fingers.

225 g (8 oz) plain flour
175 g (6 oz) block margarine
100 g (4 oz) sugar
2 teaspoons grated lemon rind
pinch of ground ginger

# Sugar Biscuits

100 g (4 oz) plain flour
100 g (4 oz) rice flour
75 g (3 oz) soft margarine
75 g (3 oz) caster sugar
1 egg yolk
1 teaspoon water
½ teaspoon vanilla essence
25 g (1 oz) granulated sugar

Put the flour and rice flour into the processor bowl with the margarine and caster sugar. Add the egg yolk, water and essence. Mix to a soft dough (plastic blade). Put on to a floured surface and roll carefully to a thin sheet, as this dough is rather delicate. Grease and flour a baking sheet. Cut the dough into shapes and put on the baking sheet. Bake at 180 °C/350 °F/Gas Mark 4 for 12 minutes. Lift carefully on to a wire rack and sprinkle with granulated sugar. For a change, substitute light soft brown sugar for caster sugar, and sprinkle with demerara sugar.

# Coffee Sandwich Biscuits

75 g (3 oz) butter
50 g (2 oz) caster sugar
75 g (3 oz) plain flour
25 g (1 oz) cornflour
2 teaspoons instant coffee
    powder
1 tablespoon water
coffee butter cream (page 140)
100 g (4 oz) icing sugar
1 teaspoon coffee essence
hot water

Cream the butter and sugar until light and fluffy (plastic blade). Add the flour, cornflour, coffee powder and water and mix to a soft dough. Put on to a floured board and roll out thinly. Cut into circles with a scone cutter. Grease a baking sheet and put the circles on it. Prick with a fork and bake at 180 °C/350 °F/Gas Mark 4 for 10 minutes. Lift off carefully and cool on a wire rack.

Put the biscuits together in pairs with coffee butter cream. Mix the icing sugar with coffee essence and just enough hot water to give a spreading consistency. Spread a little icing on top of each biscuit and leave until set.

*Chocolate Sandwich Biscuits*
Omit coffee powder and substitute 15 g (½ oz) cocoa for the same amount of flour. Put biscuits together with chocolate butter cream and top with a little melted plain chocolate.

# Honey Lemon Cookies

100 g (4 oz) soft margarine
100 g (4 oz) caster sugar
1 egg
4 tablespoons clear honey
250 g (9 oz) plain flour
1 teaspoon baking powder
pinch of salt
50 g (2 oz) chopped mixed
    candied peel
6 tablespoons lemon curd

Cream the margarine and sugar until just mixed (plastic blade). Add the egg and honey and mix until incorporated. Add the flour, baking powder and salt and process to a soft dough. Grease a baking sheet and put heaped teaspoonfuls of the mixture on to it. Flatten the tops with a fork dipped in cold water. Put a little peel on top of half the biscuits. Bake at 180 °C/350 °F/Gas Mark 4 for 20 minutes. Lift carefully on to a wire rack to cool. When cold, sandwich pairs of biscuits together with lemon curd, with peel-topped biscuits on top.

# Pineapple Cookies

Drain the pineapple and chop finely (metal blade). Keep on one side. Put the flour, baking powder and salt into the processor bowl. Cut the lard into small pieces and add to the bowl with the peanut butter. Process until the mixture is like breadcrumbs (plastic blade). Add the sugar and egg and mix until smooth. Add the pineapple and mix just long enough to incorporate. Grease a baking sheet and put heaped teaspoonfuls of the mixture on to it. Cut the cherries into small pieces and put a piece on top of each cookie. Bake at 190 °C/ 375 °F/Gas Mark 5 for 20 minutes. Lift carefully on to a wire rack to cool.

225 g (8 oz) canned pineapple rings
225 g (8 oz) plain flour
1 teaspoon baking powder
$\frac{1}{2}$ teaspoon salt
40 g (1$\frac{1}{2}$ oz) lard
6 tablespoons peanut butter
175 g (6 oz) caster sugar
1 egg
12 glacé cherries

# Almond Paste

Mix the almonds, icing sugar, caster sugar, lemon juice and essence just long enough for them to be well blended (plastic blade). In a bowl beat the egg lightly with a fork. With the machine running, add the egg through the feeder tube until the mixture blends into a firm paste. Do not overwork the paste or the oil will run out and discolour any icing placed on top. Two eggs may be necessary if they are small. Egg yolks may be used for almond paste (and the whites used for a royal icing) but this gives a dark yellow paste. For a pale and delicate almond paste, use egg whites only.

225 g (8 oz) ground almonds
100 g (4 oz) icing sugar
100 g (4 oz) caster sugar
1 teaspoon lemon juice
1 teaspoon almond essence
1 egg

# Fluffy Icing

The butter should be soft but not melted. Put into the processor bowl with the rind, and cream until just mixed (plastic blade). Add half the sugar and process until mixed. Add the juice and water and the remaining sugar and continue processing until light and fluffy.

40 g (1$\frac{1}{2}$ oz) unsalted butter
1 tablespoon grated orange or lemon rind
450 g (1 lb) icing sugar
2 tablespoons orange or lemon juice
1 tablespoon water

# Butter Cream

175 g (6 oz) butter
350 g (12 oz) icing sugar
flavouring

The butter should be soft but not melted. Sieve the icing sugar and mix with butter and flavouring (see below) until light and fluffy (plastic blade). This is enough butter cream for filling and topping a 2-layer sandwich cake.

*Vanilla*
Add 1 teaspoon vanilla essence to the mixture.

*Lemon*
Add 1 teaspoon lemon rind and 1 tablespoon lemon juice.

*Orange*
Add 1 teaspoon orange rind and 2 tablespoons orange juice.

*Coffee*
Add 2 teaspoons coffee essence.

*Chocolate*
Add 1 tablespoon cocoa dissolved in 1 tablespoon hot water.

# 11. Sauces

A good sauce enhances a dish – salad is not complete without a dressing or mayonnaise, while a meat dish often needs the complement of a gravy. With a food processor, a much wider range of sauces can be prepared by even an inexperienced cook, and time is saved by its speed.

If a savoury or sweet sauce has been made by hand and then proves lumpy, it may be quickly smoothed by using the plastic blade or blender attachment. It is far quicker however to prepare the sauces with the aid of the processor. Flour-based sauces may be mixed in the processor before heating, which speeds up the cooking and keeps the sauce smooth. Emulsified sauces such as hollandaise and mayonnaise which require the slow addition of melted butter or oil can be safely made in the processor as the liquid can be poured very slowly through the feeder tube as the machine is running – this 2-handed processing is difficult without a machine. Even a simple oil-and-vinegar salad dressing is improved by mixing in the processor, which completely emulsifies the ingredients.

## Basic White Sauce

Mix butter, flour and milk until smooth (plastic blade). Pour into a pan, bring to the boil and simmer for 3 minutes, stirring all the time. Season to taste. If a flavoured sauce is needed (see below and overleaf), prepare the additional ingredients in the processor before making the sauce.

25 g (1 oz) melted butter
25 g (1 oz) plain flour
300 ml (½ pint) milk
salt and white pepper

*Cheese Sauce*
Stir 75 g (3 oz) grated or chopped cheese into sauce just before serving.

*Egg Sauce*
Stir 2 shelled and chopped hard-boiled eggs into cooked sauce.

*Onion Sauce*
Cook 1 finely chopped medium onion in the sauce. Flavour with a pinch of ground nutmeg.

*Parsley Sauce*
Stir 2 large chopped sprigs of parsley into cooked sauce.

*Shrimp Sauce*
Add 75 g (3 oz) peeled, finely chopped shrimps to the cooked sauce and season with a few drops of Tabasco sauce.

# Basic Brown Sauce

2 rashers streaky bacon
1 onion
1 celery stick
1 carrot
4 large mushrooms
2 tablespoons oil
25 g (1 oz) plain flour
450 ml (¾ pint) beef stock
2 tablespoons tomato purée
1 bay leaf
1 sprig of parsley
salt and pepper

Derind the bacon and chop finely (metal blade). Peel the onion and chop finely (metal blade). Wash and trim the celery, peel the carrot, wipe the mushrooms and chop them finely (metal blade). Heat the oil and stir in the bacon and vegetables. Stir over low heat until the onions are soft and golden. Add the flour and stir well for 2 minutes over low heat. Add the stock gradually and then the remaining ingredients. Bring to the boil, cover and simmer for 45 minutes. Take out the bay leaf and parsley. Blend the sauce until smooth (blender attachment). Return to the pan and simmer for 10 minutes. Use for meat dishes.

# Gooseberry Sauce

225 g (8 oz) green gooseberries
2 tablespoons water
25 g (1 oz) butter
25 g (1 oz) sugar
pinch of ground allspice

Top and tail the gooseberries. Chop them finely (metal blade). Put into a pan with the water and simmer for 5 minutes. Cool slightly. Mix with the butter, sugar and spice until smooth (plastic blade). Return to a clean pan and reheat. Serve with mackerel or other oily fish.

# Curry Sauce

Peel the onion and chop finely (metal blade). Cook over low heat in the oil, until soft and golden. Stir in the flour, curry powder and paste and continue cooking for 3 minutes. Add the stock and simmer over low heat for 10 minutes. Peel and core the apple and chop finely (metal blade). Add to the sauce with the sultanas, lemon juice, salt and pepper. Simmer for 10 minutes. If a smooth sauce is preferred, blend before adding sultanas and seasonings (blender attachment). Serve with cooked meat, poultry, fish, seafood or eggs.

1 onion
1 tablespoon oil
25 g (1 oz) plain flour
15 g ($\frac{1}{2}$ oz) curry powder
1 teaspoon curry paste
450 ml ($\frac{3}{4}$ pint) beef or chicken stock
1 eating apple
50 g (2 oz) sultanas
2 teaspoons lemon juice
salt and pepper

# Bread Sauce with Onion

Peel the onion and chop finely (metal blade). Put into a pan with the milk and cloves and bring slowly to boiling point. Leave to stand in a warm place for 30 minutes. Discard the crusts from the bread and make the bread into crumbs (metal blade). Stir the crumbs into the milk and simmer for 5 minutes. Stir in the butter, salt, pepper and cream and serve at once. This is more strongly flavoured than the usual bread sauce and is very good with chicken, game or sausages.

1 small onion
300 ml ($\frac{1}{2}$ pint) milk
pinch of ground cloves
100 g (4 oz) day-old white bread
25 g (1 oz) butter
salt and pepper
2 tablespoons single cream

# Wine and Mushroom Sauce

Peel the onion and chop it finely (metal blade). Melt the butter and cook the onion until soft and golden. Wipe the mushrooms and chop finely (metal blade). Add to the onion and stir over low heat for 2 minutes. Add the stock, wine and Worcestershire sauce, stir well and simmer for 10 minutes. Cool slightly and return to the processor bowl. Mix the cornflour with the water and add to the bowl. Add salt and pepper. Mix until smooth (plastic blade). Return to the pan and simmer for 5 minutes. Serve with steak or roast beef.

1 onion
15 g ($\frac{1}{2}$ oz) butter
175 g (6 oz) button mushrooms
300 ml ($\frac{1}{2}$ pint) stock
150 ml ($\frac{1}{4}$ pint) red wine
1 tablespoon Worcestershire sauce
15 g ($\frac{1}{2}$ oz) cornflour
1 tablespoon water
salt and pepper

# Sweet and Sour Sauce

1 small onion
3 canned pineapple rings
40 g (1½ oz) sugar
15 g (½ oz) cornflour
2 tablespoons vinegar
2 teaspoons soy sauce
2 teaspoons tomato purée
pinch of salt
300 ml (½ pint) water

Peel the onion. Cut the pineapple into pieces and add to the onion. Chop finely (metal blade) and keep on one side. Mix the sugar, cornflour, vinegar, soy sauce, tomato purée, salt and water until smooth (plastic blade). Pour into a pan and simmer gently over low heat, stirring until the sauce thickens. Add the onion and pineapple and continue simmering for 3 minutes. Serve with pork or chicken.

# Tomato Sauce

1 onion
1 garlic clove
1 tablespoon oil
25 g (1 oz) plain flour
450 g (1 lb) canned tomatoes
1 teaspoon salt
1 teaspoon sugar
1 tablespoon vinegar
1 tablespoon tomato purée
pinch of dried mixed herbs
1 bay leaf
pinch of pepper

Peel the onion and garlic clove and chop finely (metal blade). Heat the oil in a pan and cook the onion and garlic until soft and golden. Work in the flour and cook for 1 minute. Put into the processor bowl. Sieve the tomatoes and their juice and add to the bowl with the salt, sugar, vinegar, tomato purée and herbs. Mix until smooth (plastic blade). Put into a pan with the bay leaf and pepper. Stir over low heat for 10 minutes. Remove the bay leaf and adjust the seasoning.

# Spaghetti Sauce

1 onion
1 garlic clove
2 tablespoons oil
1 carrot
675 g (1½ lb) chuck steak
1 chicken liver
100 g (4 oz) button mushrooms
25 g (1 oz) plain flour
225 g (8 oz) canned tomatoes
300 ml (½ pint) beef stock
4 tablespoons red wine
4 tablespoons tomato purée
½ teaspoon dried mixed herbs
salt and pepper

Peel the onion and garlic clove and chop finely (metal blade). Heat the oil in a pan and stir in the onion and garlic until soft and golden. Peel the carrot and chop finely (metal blade). Add to the onion and cook for 3 minutes. Cut the steak and liver into pieces and chop finely (metal blade). Add to the pan and continue cooking until lightly browned. Wipe the mushrooms and chop finely (metal blade). Add to the pan and cook for 2 minutes. Drain off surplus fat from the pan. Work in the flour and cook for 1 minute. Drain the tomatoes and add juice to the pan. Cut tomatoes and remove seeds. Chop the flesh finely (metal blade) and add to the pan. Stir in the remaining ingredients and bring to the boil. Cover, lower heat and simmer for 1 hour. Serve with any pasta.

# Vinaigrette Sauce

Mix all the ingredients until well blended (plastic blade). Use for green salads, tomatoes, cold leeks, asparagus, globe artichokes and avocados.

4 tablespoons oil
2 tablespoons wine vinegar
½ teaspoon salt
½ teaspoon caster sugar
½ teaspoon mustard powder
pinch of pepper

# Blue Cheese Salad Dressing

Chop the blue cheese in small pieces (metal blade). Add the other ingredients and process until smooth (plastic blade). Chill and serve on a green salad.

50 g (2 oz) Danish blue cheese
100 g (4 oz) cottage cheese
3 tablespoons mayonnaise
2 tablespoons single cream
1 teaspoon French mustard
2 teaspoons lemon juice
1 teaspoon chopped chives

# Hollandaise Sauce

Mix the egg yolks, lemon juice, water, salt and pepper until just blended (plastic blade). Melt the butter without browning. With the machine running, pour the butter slowly through the feeder tube until completely mixed in and the sauce is thick. Serve immediately with fish, asparagus, artichokes or other vegetables.

3 egg yolks
1 tablespoon lemon juice
1 tablespoon warm water
salt and white pepper
100 g (4 oz) unsalted butter

*Maltaise Sauce*
Stir in 1 teaspoon grated orange rind and 1 tablespoon orange juice and serve with vegetables.

*Mousseline Sauce*
Before preparing Hollandaise Sauce, whip 150 ml (¼ pint) double cream to soft peaks and keep on one side. Prepare sauce and fold in the cream. Serve with fish, vegetables or eggs.

1. Egg, egg yolk and seasoning ready for mixing

2. Adding oil through feeder tube (metal then plastic blades)

3. Mayonnaise after addition of vinegar or lemon juice

# Mayonnaise

1 egg and 1 egg yolk
½ teaspoon mustard powder
salt and white pepper
300 ml (½ pint) oil
1 tablespoon wine vinegar or
    lemon juice

Mix the egg, egg yolk, mustard, salt and pepper until smooth (metal blade). With the machine running (metal blade) pour half the oil slowly through the feeder tube. Switch off the machine to change blades. Add the remaining oil through the feeder tube and mix until the mayonnaise is thick (plastic blade). Add vinegar or lemon juice and process until mixed.

*Green Mayonnaise*
Add 1 chopped garlic clove and 1 tablespoon each finely chopped parsley, chives and basil to the mayonnaise. Process just long enough to blend.

*Curry Mayonnaise*
Add 1 tablespoon tomato purée, 1 tablespoon curry paste, 1 teaspoon lemon juice and 2 tablespoons double cream to the mayonnaise. Process just long enough to blend.

*Niçoise Mayonnaise*
Add 1 chopped garlic clove and ½ teaspoon chopped tarragon with 2 tablespoons tomato purée to the mayonnaise. Process to blend.

# Custard Sauce

1 egg
50 g (2 oz) caster sugar
25 g (1 oz) butter
½ teaspoon vanilla essence
600 ml (1 pint) milk
25 g (1 oz) cornflour

Mix the egg, sugar, butter and essence until creamy (plastic blade). Mix 3 tablespoons milk with the cornflour. Heat the rest of the milk to boiling point. Pour on to the cornflour and return to the pan. Cook for 2 minutes over low heat, stirring all the time. With the machine running, pour the milk mixture slowly through the feeder tube and continue processing until smooth. Serve hot or cold.

# Confectioner's Custard

2 egg yolks
50 g (2 oz) sugar
25 g (1 oz) plain flour
300 ml (½ pint) milk
15 g (½ oz) unsalted butter
few drops of vanilla essence

Mix the egg yolks, sugar, flour and half the milk until smooth (plastic blade). With the machine running, add the remaining milk through the feeder tube until blended. Put into a thick pan and cook gently over low heat, stirring well until thick. Remove from the heat, add butter and essence and cool. Use for cake filling, choux buns or the base of fruit flans. For a lighter filling, mix the cold custard with an equal quantity of softly whipped double cream (whisk attachment). The custard may be flavoured with a liqueur or a little coffee essence.

# Chocolate Fudge Sauce

25 g (1 oz) plain chocolate
2 tablespoons milk
1 tablespoon golden syrup
15 g (½ oz) butter
100 g (4 oz) light soft brown
  sugar
½ teaspoon vanilla essence

Grate the chocolate (disc A). Warm the milk, syrup and butter in a small pan until the butter has just melted. Add to the chocolate and process until smooth (plastic blade). Return to the pan with the sugar and stir over low heat until the sugar has dissolved. Bring to the boil and boil without stirring for 3 minutes. Add the essence and serve hot with puddings or ice cream.

# Rum Butter

225 g (8 oz) unsalted butter
225 g (8 oz) light soft brown
  sugar
6 tablespoons light rum

Cut the butter into small pieces and process until soft (plastic blade). Add half the sugar and process until light and fluffy. With the machine running add the remaining sugar and the rum in small amounts through the feeder tube until well mixed. This must be done slowly or the mixture may curdle. Put into a serving dish and chill. Serve with puddings or mince pies, or as a spread on biscuits.

# 12. Preserves and Pickles

Besides being full of flavour, home-made preserves and pickles can be very economical. Prepared from surplus garden produce or from cheap seasonal ingredients from markets, the savings can be considerable. The only drawback used to be the long hours spent chopping and shredding vegetables and fruit. Now, with the food processor, these preparations are easily completed. Once the ingredients have been washed and weighed and the jars sterilised, marmalade, mincemeat, chutney and pickles are little trouble to make.

Use a large saucepan or preserving pan for cooking the ingredients, and stir with a wooden spoon. When making jam or marmalade, the ingredients must be cooked long enough to reduce the liquid by evaporation (the mixture should be reduced by half). When the sugar is added, it must be dissolved completely over low heat and then the mixture boiled rapidly to setting point.

Chutney ingredients must be cooked until very soft and the finished mixture should be soft and golden and of the consistency of jam.

All jars should be sterilised with boiling water and thoroughly dried. Jam may be covered with plastic or metal lids or transparent covers, but chutney and pickles must be covered with vinegar-proof lids to prevent evaporation.

# Chunky Marmalade

1·5 kg (3 lb) Seville oranges
2 lemons
3·5 litres (6 pints) water
3 kg (6 lb) sugar

Scrub the oranges and lemons and cut them into small pieces, being sure to save any juice. Remove the pips and tie them in a muslin bag. Chop the fruit coarsely (metal blade). Put into a preserving pan with any juice which has run out. Add the water and the bag of pips. Bring to the boil and then simmer for about 1½ hours until the peel is soft and the quantity of mixture reduced to a half. Remove the bag of pips and squeeze out liquid into the pan. Stir in the sugar and heat gently until it has dissolved. Bring to the boil rapidly and then boil hard to setting point, which will take about 20 minutes. The marmalade is ready when a little placed on a cold saucer sets quickly and wrinkles if pushed with a finger. Remove from the heat at once and leave to stand for 15 minutes. Skim with a slotted spoon, and then stir thoroughly to distribute the peel. Pour into warm sterilised jars and cover when cold.

# Three Fruit Marmalade

2 sweet oranges
4 lemons
2 grapefruit
3·5 litres (6 pints) water
3 kg (6 lb) sugar

Scrub the oranges and lemons and cut them into small pieces and remove the pips. Peel the grapefruit and scrape off all the white pith from the skin and from the fruit. Cut the fruit and peel into pieces, and remove the pips. Tie all the pips into a small muslin bag. Chop the fruit and peel coarsely (metal blade). Put all the fruit and peel into a preserving pan with any juice which has run out and add the water and the bag of pips. Bring to the boil and then simmer for about 1½ hours until the peel is soft and the quantity of mixture reduced to a half. Take out the bag of pips and squeeze any liquid into the pan. Stir in the sugar over low heat until dissolved and then boil rapidly to setting point, which will take about 20 minutes. The marmalade is ready when a little placed on a cold saucer sets quickly and wrinkles if pushed with a finger. Remove from the heat at once and leave to stand for 15 minutes. Skim with a slotted spoon, and then stir thoroughly to distribute the peel. Pour into warm sterilised jars and cover when cold.

# Golden Jam

Peel and core the apples and pears and tie the peel and cores into a large piece of muslin. Chop the flesh coarsely (metal blade). Put the flesh into a preserving pan with the cider and the muslin bag and simmer for 40 minutes. The fruit should be soft but with some pieces still whole. Take out the muslin bag and squeeze thoroughly to return all the juice to the pan. Stir in the sugar and heat gently, stirring until the sugar has dissolved. Add the ginger and bring to the boil. Boil rapidly to setting point. The jam is ready when a little dropped on a cold saucer sets quickly and wrinkles if pushed with a finger. Cool for 5 minutes, stir well, pour into warm sterilised jars and cover.

1·5 kg (3 lb) cooking apples
1·5 kg (3 lb) eating pears
1·2 litres (2 pints) dry cider
2 kg (4 lb) sugar
¼ teaspoon ground ginger

# Cranberry and Orange Preserve

This is a good preserve to make around Christmas time when fresh cranberries are plentiful. It is suitable for eating with turkey, pork or ham, and looks attractive if served in the hollowed-out skins of oranges. It also makes a delicious filling for small tarts or sponge cakes. Put the cranberries into the cold water and simmer until the skins break. Cool slightly. Put cranberries and liquid into bowl and chop finely (metal blade). Return to the pan. Peel the orange and remove the pips. Chop the flesh finely (metal blade). Add to the cranberries. Chop the walnuts coarsely (metal blade) and keep on one side. Add the sugar, raisins and boiling water to the fruit, bring to the boil and simmer for 20 minutes. Stir the walnuts into the mixture and cool for 10 minutes. Stir well, put into small, warm, sterilised jars and cover.

450 g (1 lb) cranberries
150 ml (¼ pint) cold water
1 orange
225 g (8 oz) walnut halves
675 g (1½ lb) sugar
100 g (4 oz) seedless raisins
6 tablespoons boiling water

# Old Fashioned Mincemeat

175 g (6 oz) cooking apples
225 g (8 oz) seedless raisins
225 g (8 oz) sultanas
225 g (8 oz) currants
100 g (4 oz) mixed candied peel
50 g (2 oz) blanched almonds
100 g (4 oz) shredded suet
225 g (8 oz) dark soft brown
   sugar
1 lemon
½ teaspoon ground mixed spice
½ teaspoon ground cinnamon

Peel and core the apples and chop them finely (metal blade). Tip into a mixing bowl. Chop raisins, sultanas and currants coarsely (metal blade). Be very careful when chopping the fruit as the machine works very quickly and the fruit should be chopped and not made into a paste. Tip into the bowl with apples. If the peel is not already chopped, chop it coarsely (metal blade). Chop the almonds coarsely (metal blade). Add to the other fruit with the suet and sugar. Grate the rind from the lemon and squeeze out the juice (juice extractor). Add the rind, juice and spices to the mincemeat. Mix thoroughly and pack into sterilised jars. Cover and store in a cool dry place.

# Mixed Mustard Pickles

1 marrow
1 cucumber
450 g (1 lb) French beans
1 cauliflower
450 g (1 lb) pickling onions
25 g (1 oz) cooking salt
300 g (10 oz) sugar
50 g (2 oz) plain flour
50 g (2 oz) mustard powder
15 g (½ oz) turmeric
15 g (½ oz) ground ginger
15 g (½ oz) ground nutmeg
1·2 litres (2 pints) vinegar

Wipe but do not peel the marrow. Remove seeds and pith. Chop coarsely (metal blade) and put into a large bowl. Wipe but do not peel the cucumber and chop it (metal blade). Top and tail the French beans and chop (metal blade). Add cucumber and French beans to the marrow. Remove green leaves from the cauliflower, and break cauliflower up into small pieces. Add to the bowl with the peeled onions. Sprinkle with the salt, cover with cold water and leave overnight. Drain off the water. Mix the sugar, flour, spices and a little of the vinegar to make a smooth paste. Put the vegetables into a pan with the remaining vinegar and simmer until just tender. Add a little of the boiling vinegar to the paste and mix well. Return to the pan and simmer for 10 minutes, stirring well. Put into warm sterilised jars and cover with vinegar-proof lids.

# Pickled Red Cabbage

Discard discoloured leaves from the cabbage. Cut the cabbage into 8 wedges and remove the hard core. Shred the cabbage (disc H). Arrange alternate layers of cabbage and salt in a bowl, cover and leave in a cool place overnight. Put the vinegar and spice into a pan, bring to the boil and then simmer for 15 minutes. Leave until cold and then strain to remove the spices. Drain the salt liquid from the cabbage. Rinse the cabbage in cold water and drain completely. Pack the cabbage into sterilised jars and pour on the cold vinegar to cover it completely. Press down the cabbage with the handle of a wooden spoon from time to time as the vinegar is poured in so that air pockets are eliminated. Cover with vinegar-proof lids. Keep for a week before using, but do not store the cabbage longer than 3 months, or it will become very soft.

1 kg (2 lb) red cabbage
225 g (8 oz) cooking salt
1·5 litres (2½ pints) vinegar
2 tablespoons whole pickling
  spice

# Rhubarb Chutney

This is a good chutney to make when rhubarb is getting older and thicker and is less attractive for table use. Wipe the rhubarb and cut into pieces. Chop coarsely (metal blade). Peel the onions and chop coarsely (metal blade). Put into a preserving pan with all the other ingredients. Simmer gently until the sugar has dissolved, stirring well. Bring to the boil and boil for 5 minutes, then reduce heat and simmer for about 1 hour until the mixture is thick and brown. Be sure to stir often to prevent sticking. Pour into warm sterilised jars and cover with vinegar-proof lids. Store in a cool, dark, dry place.

1 kg (2 lb) rhubarb
225 g (8 oz) onions
225 g (8 oz) sultanas
675 g (1½ lb) dark soft brown
  sugar
600 ml (1 pint) vinegar
15 g (½ oz) mustard powder
1 teaspoon ground mixed spice
1 teaspoon ground ginger
1 teaspoon salt
1 teaspoon pepper
¼ teaspoon cayenne pepper

# Red Tomato Chutney

Peel the onions, cut them in pieces and then chop coarsely (metal blade). Tip into a large, heavy-based pan. Skin the tomatoes by dipping them in boiling water. Cut into quarters and then chop coarsely (metal blade). Put into the pan with all the other ingredients. Bring to the boil and then simmer without a lid for about 1 hour until thick, stirring occasionally. Pour into warm sterilised jars and cover with vinegar-proof lids. Store in a cool, dark, dry place.

450 g (1 lb) onions
2·5 kg (5 lb) ripe tomatoes
300 ml (½ pint) vinegar
350 g (12 oz) sugar
15 g (½ oz) salt
1 teaspoon cayenne pepper
1 teaspoon mustard powder
1 teaspoon ground allspice

1. Apples and onions ready for chopping

2. Skinning tomatoes

3. Adding sugar to preserving pan

# Apple Mint Chutney

1 kg (2 lb) cooking apples
1 kg (2 lb) onions
450 g (1 lb) red tomatoes
8 tablespoons mint leaves
3 large sprigs of parsley
225 g (8 oz) sultanas
2 lemons
450 g (1 lb) dark soft brown
   sugar
600 ml (1 pint) white vinegar
2 teaspoons salt
2 teaspoons ground mixed
   spice

Peel and core the apples and cut them in quarters. Peel the onions and cut them into large pieces. Chop the apples and onions (metal blade). Skin the tomatoes by dipping them into boiling water. Chop the tomatoes (metal blade) and chop the mint and parsley (metal blade). Put the apples, onions, tomatoes and herbs into a large preserving pan. Add the sultanas. Grate the rind from the lemons and extract the juice (juice extractor). Add the rind and juice to the pan with the sugar, vinegar, salt and spices. Stir over low heat until the sugar has dissolved. Bring to the boil, then simmer gently, stirring occasionally, for about 1½ hours until the chutney is thick and brown. Pour into warm sterilised jars and cover with vinegar-proof lids. Store in a cool, dark, dry place.

# Pepper and Tomato Chutney

4 large red peppers
4 large green peppers
675 g (1½ lb) green tomatoes
3 cucumbers
2 large onions
40 g (1½ oz) cooking salt
225 g (8 oz) hard white cabbage
750 ml (1¼ pints) vinegar
100 g (4 oz) dark soft brown
   sugar
2 teaspoons mustard powder
2 teaspoons ground ginger
1 teaspoon turmeric
1 teaspoon ground cinnamon
½ teaspoon ground mace
3 bay leaves

Remove the stems and seeds from the peppers and cut the flesh into large pieces. Skin the tomatoes by dipping them into boiling water. Cut the tomatoes into quarters. Wipe but do not peel the cucumbers and cut them into chunks. Peel the onions and cut them into small pieces. Chop all these vegetables finely (metal blade), sprinkle with salt and leave to stand for 1 hour. Put them into a colander to drain, pressing out the salt liquid which will have formed. Shred the cabbage (disc H). Mix all the vegetables together and put into a preserving pan with the vinegar and sugar. Heat slowly to simmering point, stirring gently. Add all the remaining ingredients and boil for 5 minutes, then reduce heat and simmer for 30 minutes. Take out the bay leaves. Pour into warm sterilised jars and cover with vinegar-proof lids. Store in a cool, dark, dry place.

# Tomato Purée for the Freezer

2 kg (4 lb) ripe tomatoes
100 g (4 oz) bacon
1 onion
1 tablespoon oil
salt and pepper
pinch of sugar
pinch of ground nutmeg
2 bay leaves

Wash the tomatoes but do not peel them. Cut them in eighths and chop coarsely (metal blade). Keep on one side. Derind the bacon and peel the onion. Chop coarsely (metal blade). Heat the oil in a pan and cook the bacon and onion for 5 minutes, stirring well until the onion is soft and golden. Add the tomatoes and stir over gentle heat for 10 minutes. Add just enough water to cover and season with salt, pepper, sugar, nutmeg and bay leaves. Cover and simmer until the tomatoes have completely disintegrated and the mixture is soft and thick. Cool slightly and remove bay leaves. Blend until creamy (blender attachment). Put through a sieve and leave the purée to cool. Put into rigid containers and cover, leaving headspace for expansion. Seal, label and freeze. This purée makes a useful base for sauces and is particularly good for sauces to be served with pasta. It may also be used as a basis for soups.

# Index